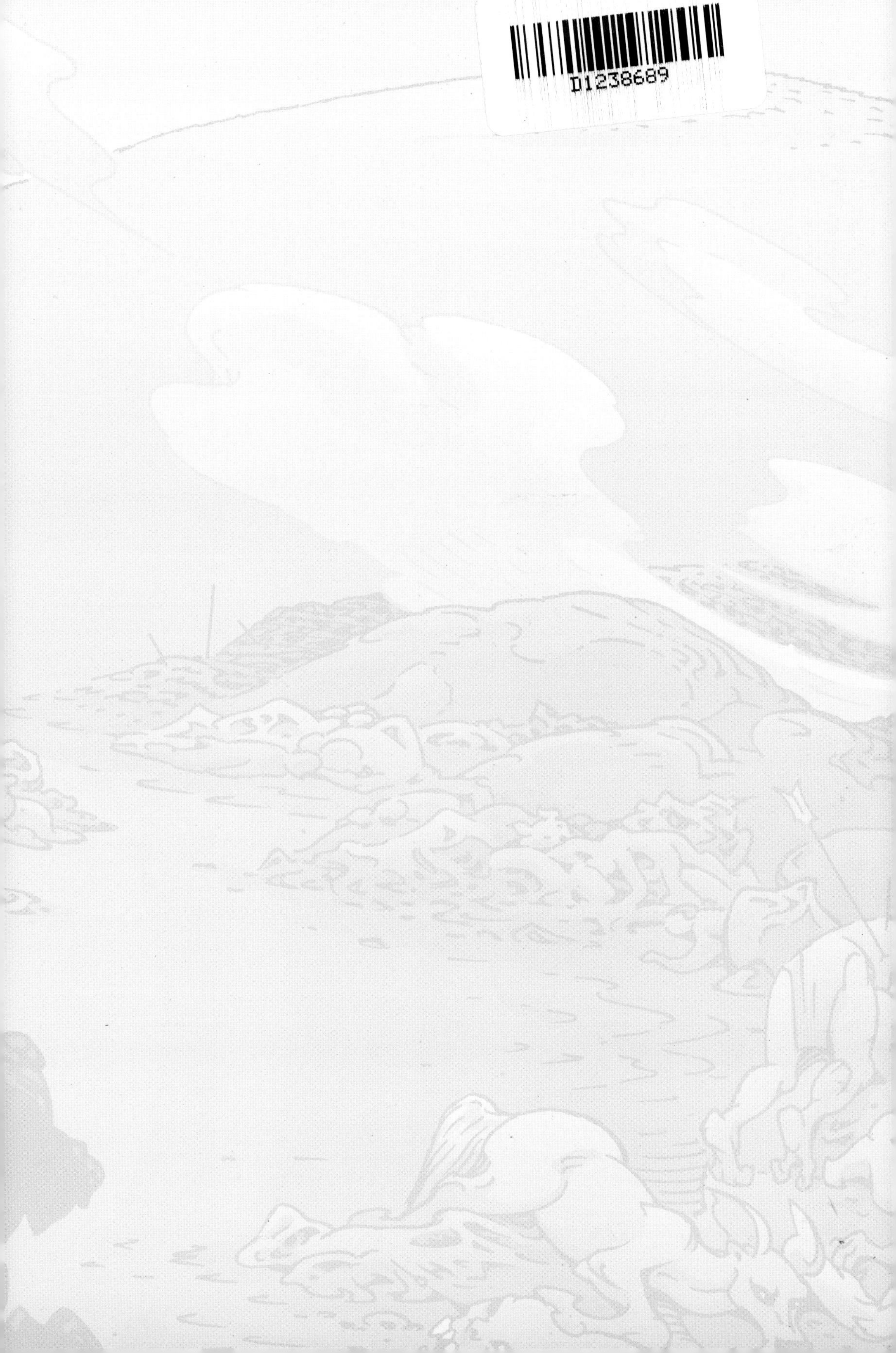

THE PROBLEM OF SUSAN

AND OTHER STORIES

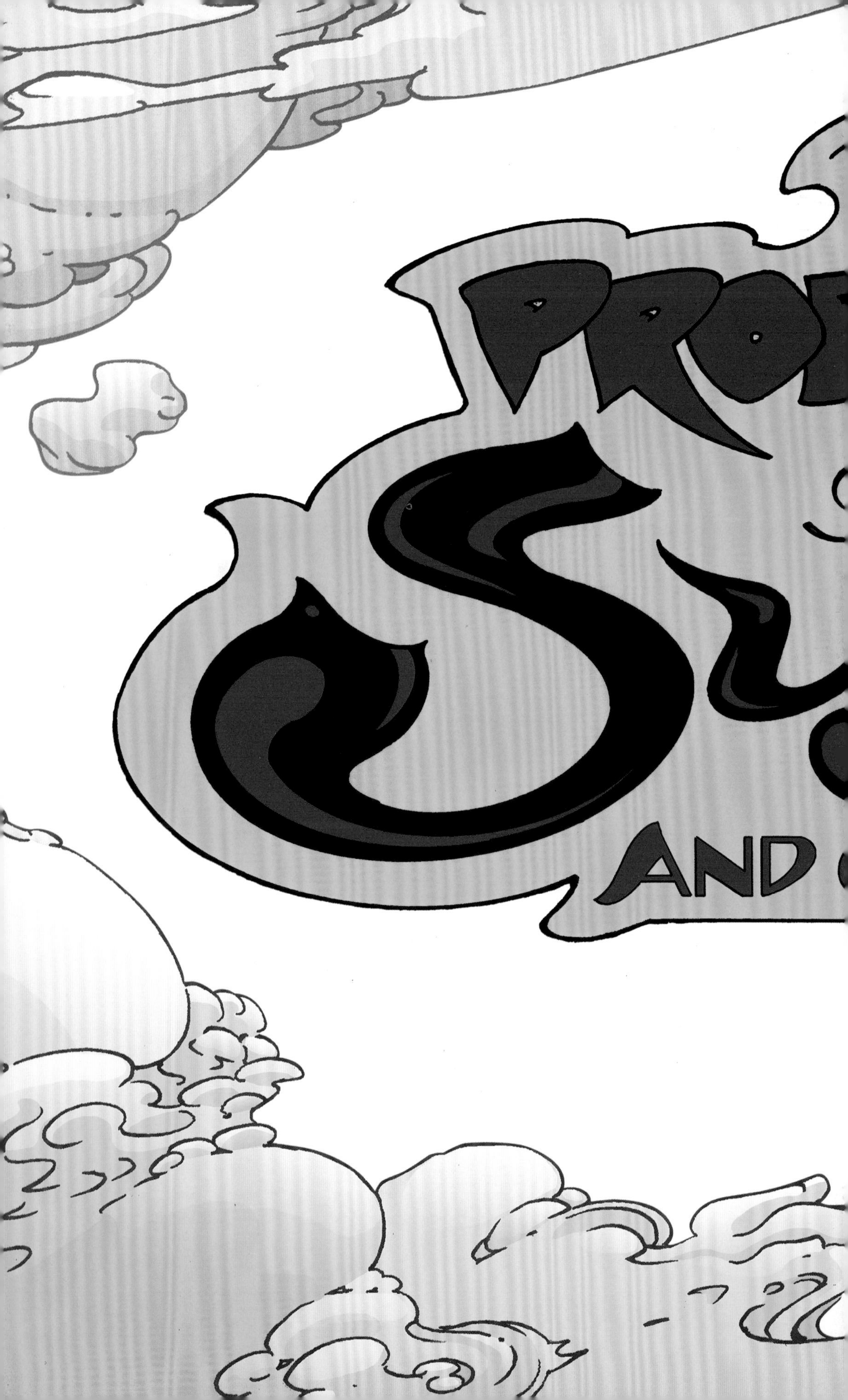
AND

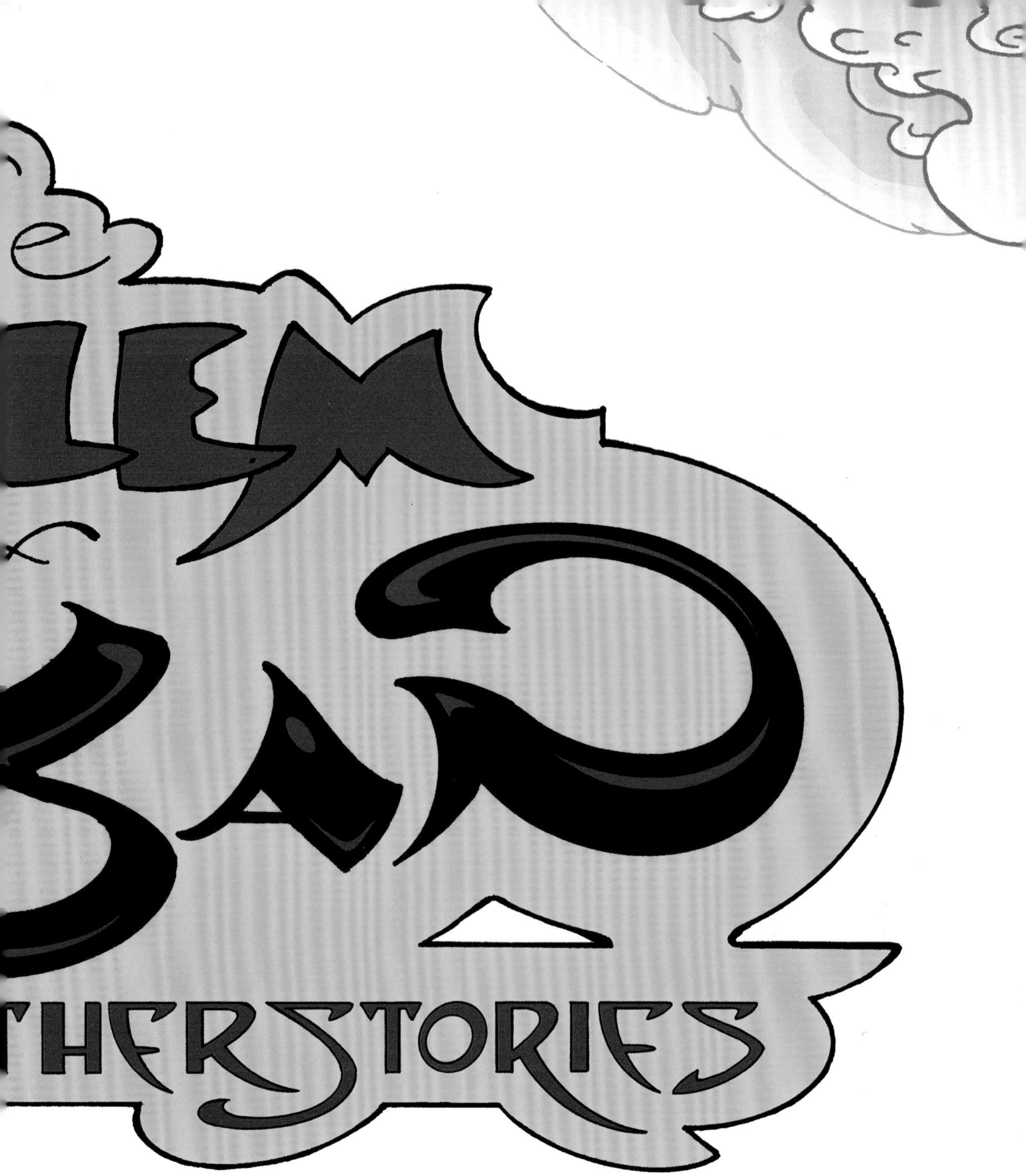
THERSTORIES

NEIL GAIMAN
Stories and words

P. CRAIG RUSSELL
Adaptation and Art *(The Problem of Susan, Locks)*
Script and Layout *(October in the Chair)*

SCOTT HAMPTON
Art *(October in the Chair)*

PAUL CHADWICK
Art *(The Day the Saucers Came)*

LOVERN KINDZIERSKI
Colors *(The Problem of Susan, Locks)*

GALEN SHOWMAN
Letters *(The Problem of Susan, Locks)*

RICK PARKER
Letters *(October in the Chair)*

GASPAR SALADINO
Letters *(The Day the Saucers Came)*

DARK HORSE BOOKS

MIKE RICHARDSON President and Publisher

DANIEL CHABON Editor

BRETT ISRAEL Assistant Editor

SARAH TERRY Designer

ADAM PRUETT Digital Art Technician

Special thanks to Diana Schutz

The Day the Saucers Came previously collected in *Dark Horse Presents* Vol. 2 #21

Published by Dark Horse Books
A division of Dark Horse Comics, Inc.
10956 SE Main Street, Milwaukie, OR 97222

DarkHorse.com

To find a comic shop in your area, check out the Comic Shop Locator Service: comicshoplocator.com

First edition: January 2019 | ISBN 978-1-50670-511-8
Digital ISBN 978-1-63008-973-3

10 9 8 7 6 5 4 3 2 1
Printed in China

Library of Congress Cataloging-in-Publication Data

Names: Gaiman, Neil, author. | Russell, P. Craig, artist. | Hampton, Scott, artist. | Chadwick, Paul (Paul H.), artist. | Kindzierski, Lovern, 1954- colourist. | Showman, Galen, letterer. | Parker, Rick, 1946- letterer. | Saladino, Gaspar, letterer.
Title: The problem of Susan and other stories / Neil Gaiman, stories and words ; P. Craig Russell, adaptation and art (The Problem of Susan, Locks) ; Scott Hampton, art (October in the Chair) ; Paul Chadwick, art (The Day the Saucers Came) ; Lovern Kindzierski, colors (The Problem of Susan, Locks) ; Galen Showman, letters (The Problem of Susan, Locks) ; Rick Parker, letters (October in the Chair) ; Gaspar Saladino, letters (The Day the Saucers Came).
Description: First edition. | Milwaukie, OR : Dark Horse Books, January 2019. | "The Day the Saucers Came previously collected in Dark Horse Presents Vol. #21"
Identifiers: LCCN 2018035576 | ISBN 9781506705118 (hardback)
Subjects: LCSH: Comic books, strips, etc. | BISAC: COMICS & GRAPHIC NOVELS / Fantasy. | COMICS & GRAPHIC NOVELS / Anthologies. | COMICS & GRAPHIC NOVELS / General.
Classification: LCC PN6737.G3 A6 2019 | DDC 741.5/942--dc23
LC record available at https://lccn.loc.gov/2018035576

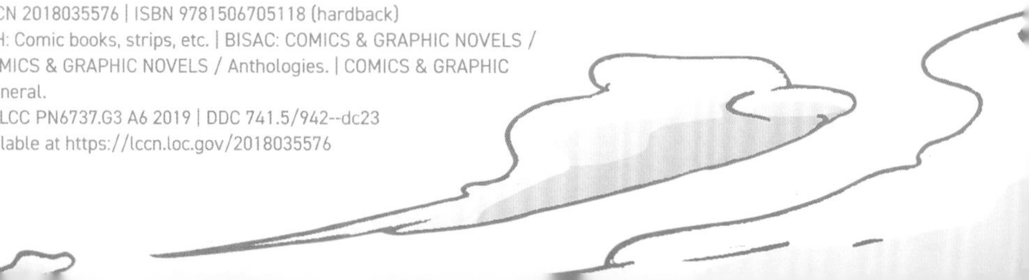

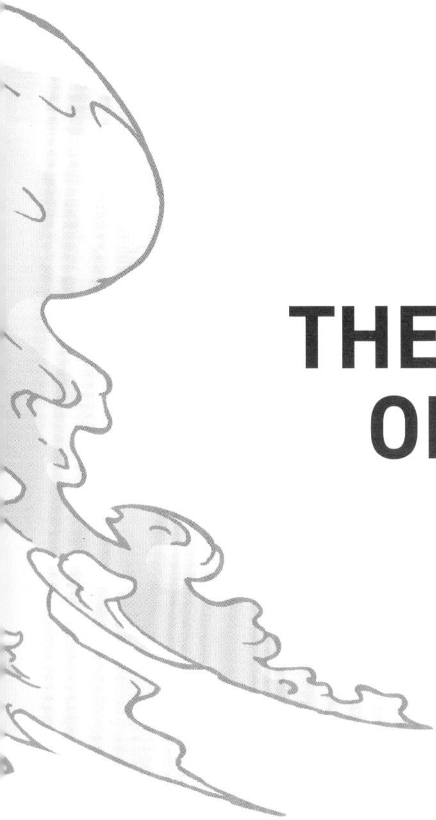

THE PROBLEM OF SUSAN

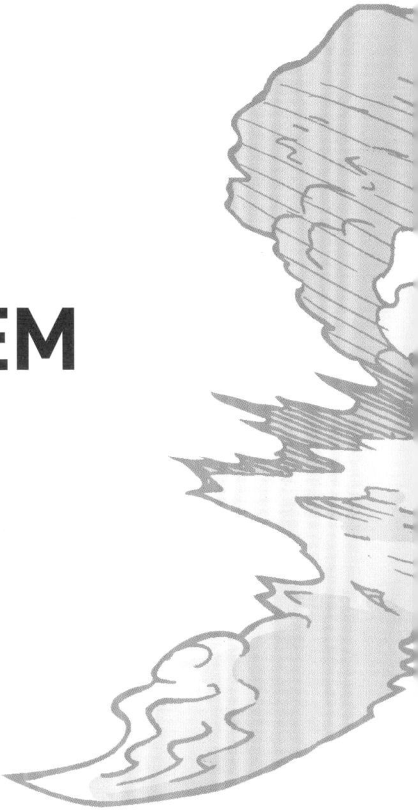

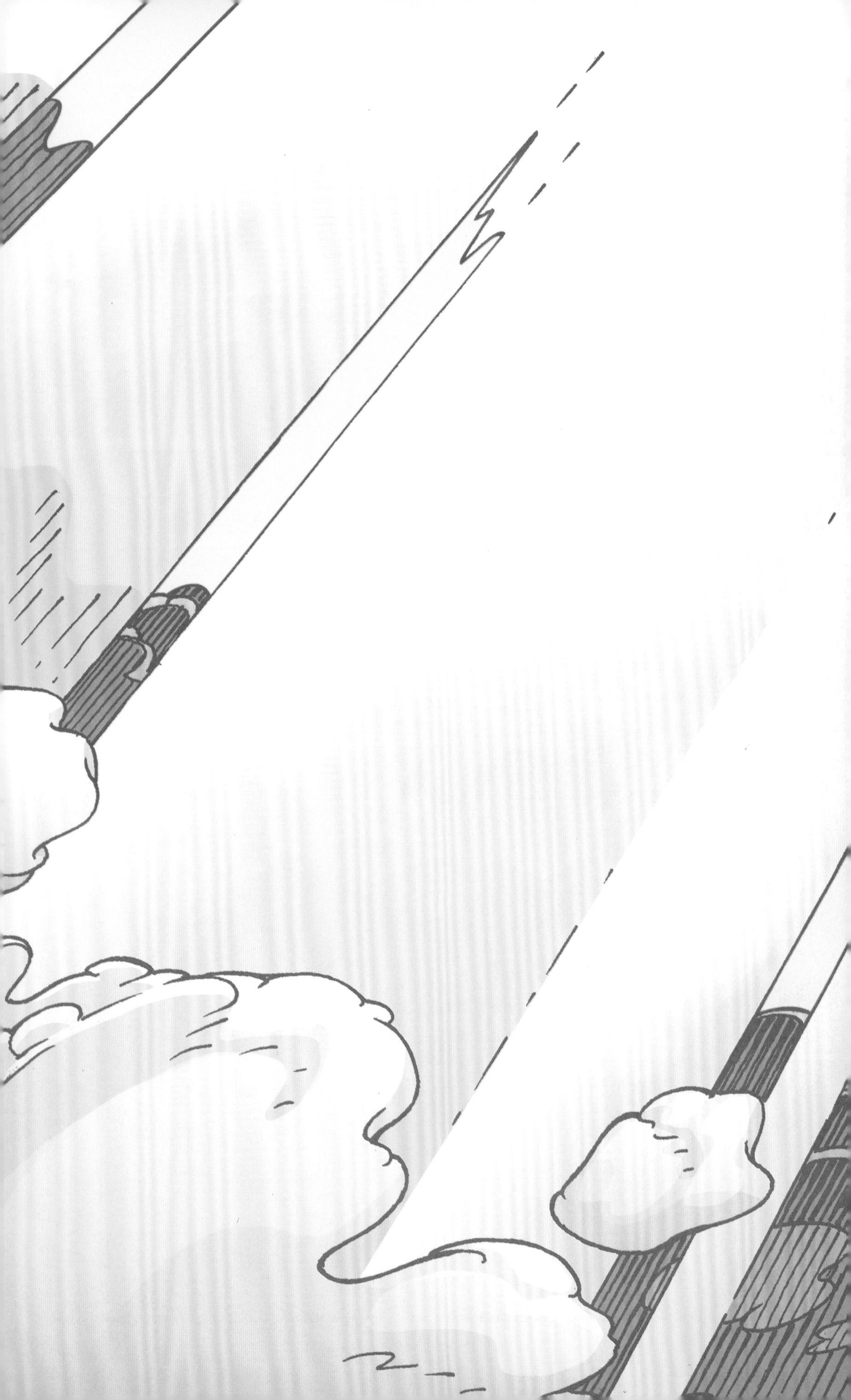

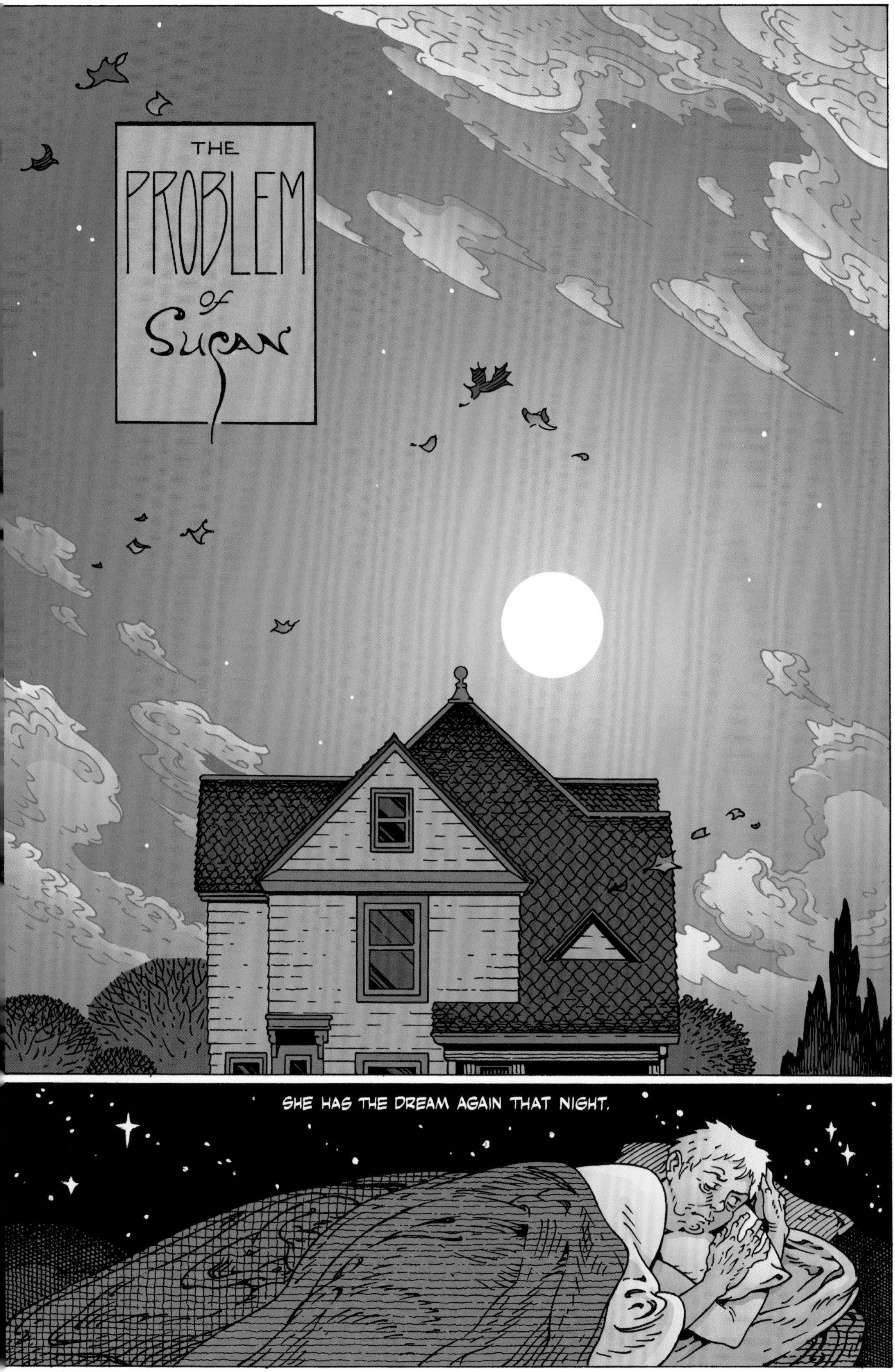
THE PROBLEM of SUSAN
SHE HAS THE DREAM AGAIN THAT NIGHT.

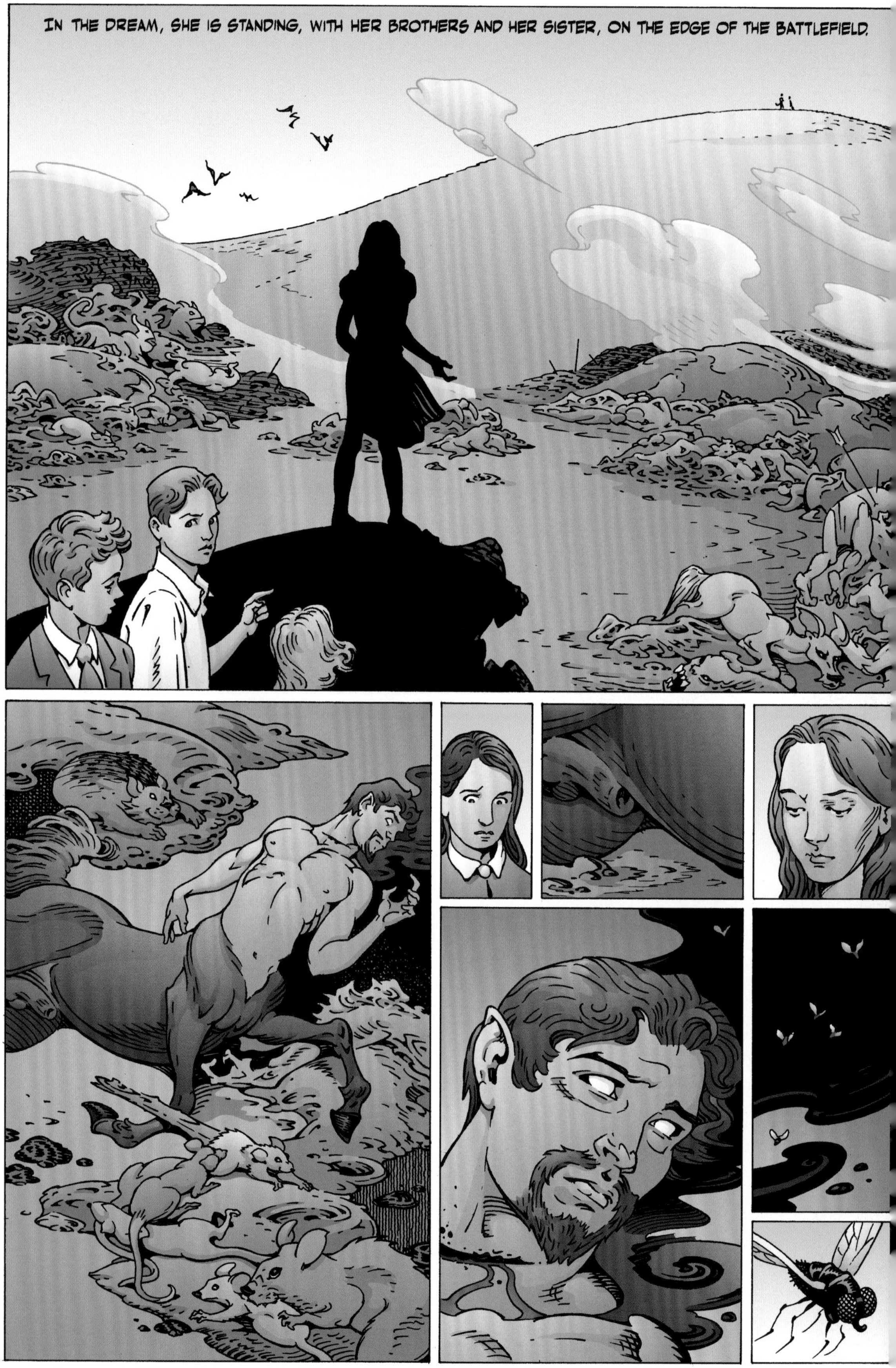
IN THE DREAM, SHE IS STANDING, WITH HER BROTHERS AND HER SISTER, ON THE EDGE OF THE BATTLEFIELD.

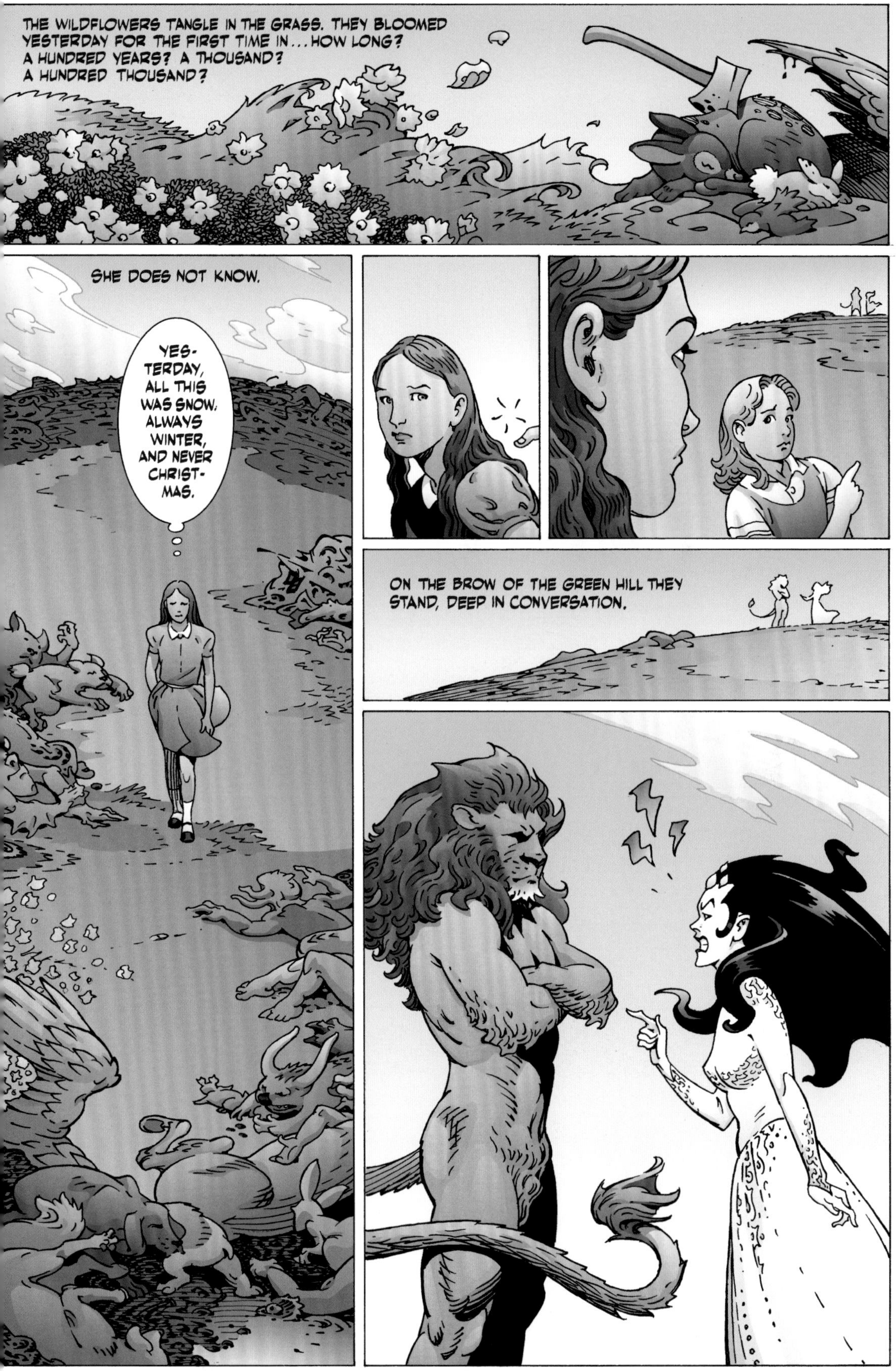
THE WILDFLOWERS TANGLE IN THE GRASS. THEY BLOOMED YESTERDAY FOR THE FIRST TIME IN... HOW LONG? A HUNDRED YEARS? A THOUSAND? A HUNDRED THOUSAND?
SHE DOES NOT KNOW.
YES-TERDAY, ALL THIS WAS SNOW, ALWAYS WINTER, AND NEVER CHRIST-MAS.
ON THE BROW OF THE GREEN HILL THEY STAND, DEEP IN CONVERSATION.

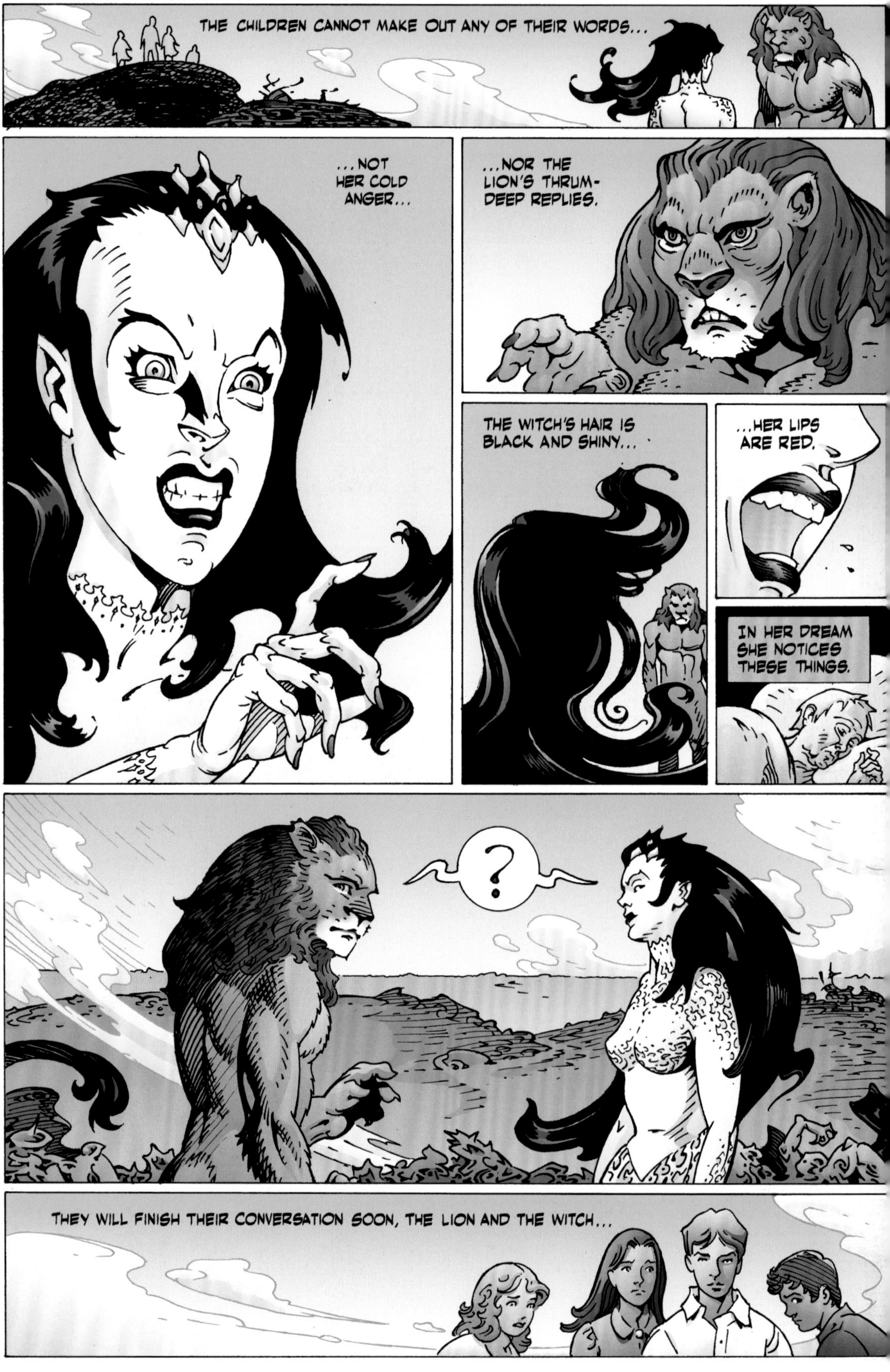
THE CHILDREN CANNOT MAKE OUT ANY OF THEIR WORDS...
...NOT HER COLD ANGER...
...NOR THE LION'S THRUM-DEEP REPLIES.
THE WITCH'S HAIR IS BLACK AND SHINY...
...HER LIPS ARE RED.
IN HER DREAM SHE NOTICES THESE THINGS.
?
THEY WILL FINISH THEIR CONVERSATION SOON, THE LION AND THE WITCH...

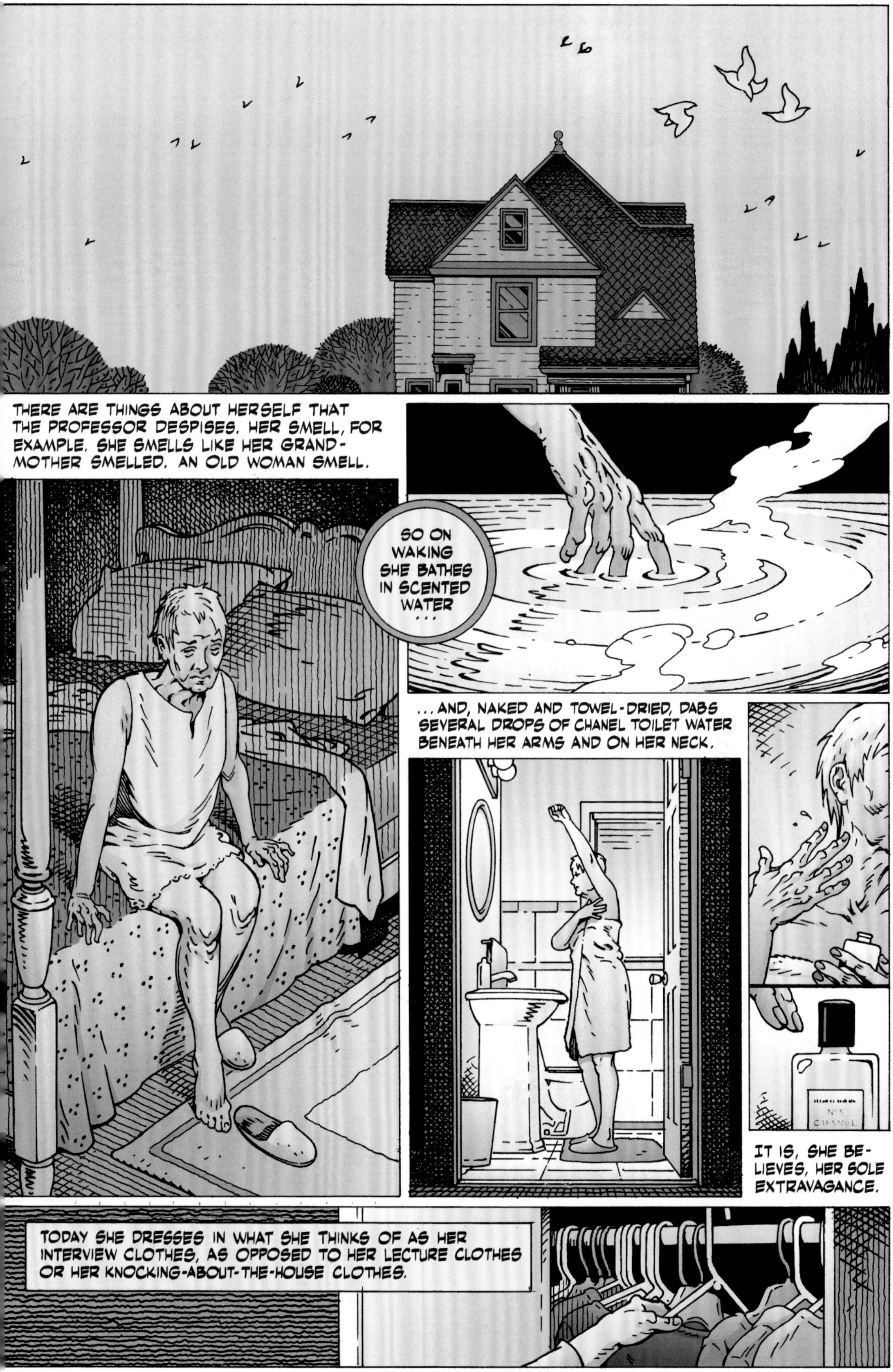
THERE ARE THINGS ABOUT HERSELF THAT THE PROFESSOR DESPISES. HER SMELL, FOR EXAMPLE. SHE SMELLS LIKE HER GRAND-MOTHER SMELLED. AN OLD WOMAN SMELL.
SO ON WAKING SHE BATHES IN SCENTED WATER . . .
. . . AND, NAKED AND TOWEL-DRIED, DABS SEVERAL DROPS OF CHANEL TOILET WATER BENEATH HER ARMS AND ON HER NECK.
IT IS, SHE BE-LIEVES, HER SOLE EXTRAVAGANCE.
TODAY SHE DRESSES IN WHAT SHE THINKS OF AS HER INTERVIEW CLOTHES, AS OPPOSED TO HER LECTURE CLOTHES OR HER KNOCKING-ABOUT-THE-HOUSE CLOTHES.

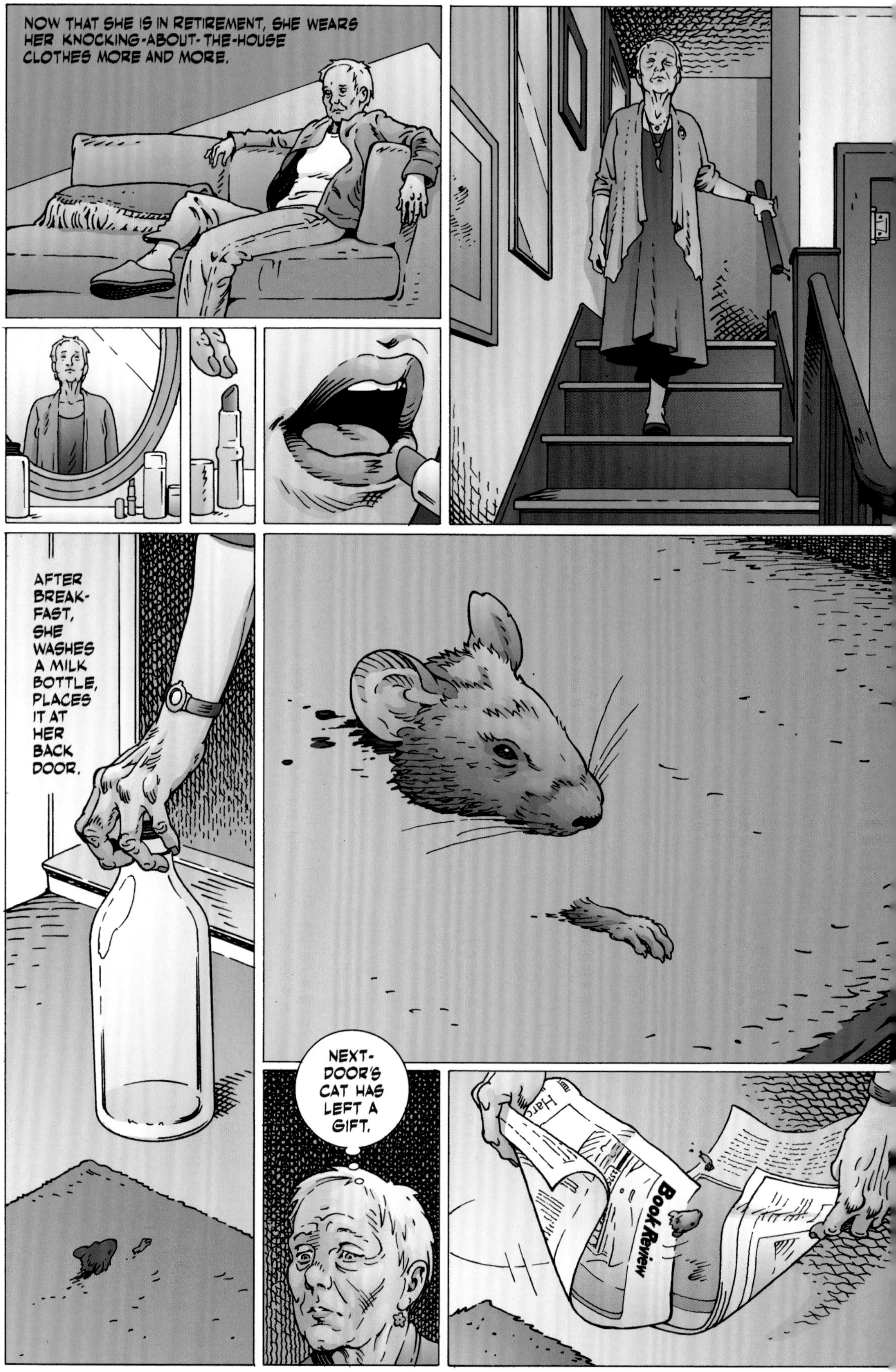
NOW THAT SHE IS IN RETIREMENT, SHE WEARS HER KNOCKING-ABOUT-THE-HOUSE CLOTHES MORE AND MORE.
AFTER BREAK-FAST, SHE WASHES A MILK BOTTLE, PLACES IT AT HER BACK DOOR.
NEXT-DOOR'S CAT HAS LEFT A GIFT.
Book Review

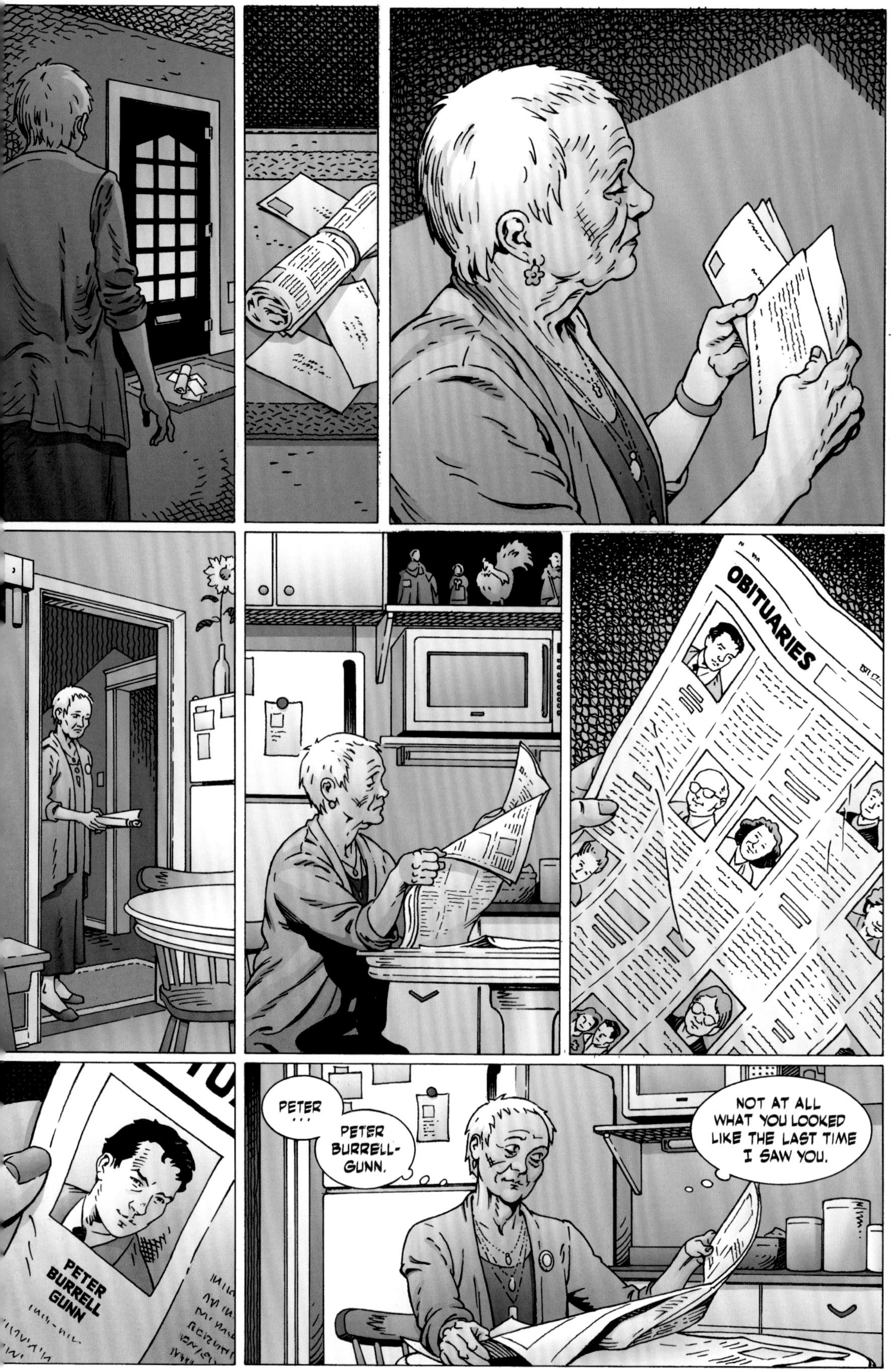
OBITUARIES
PETER BURRELL GUNN
PETER . . .
PETER BURRELL-GUNN.
NOT AT ALL WHAT YOU LOOKED LIKE THE LAST TIME I SAW YOU.

THAT HAD BEEN AT A *LITERARY MONTHLY* CHRISTMAS PARTY AND HE HAD REMINDED HER OF NOTHING SO MUCH AS...

A CARI-CATURE OF AN OWL.

IN THE PHOTOGRAPH, HE IS VERY BEAUTIFUL. HE LOOKS WILD, AND NOBLE.

SHE HAD SPENT AN EVENING ONCE KISSING HIM IN A SUMMER HOUSE, ALTHOUGH SHE CANNOT REMEMBER FOR THE LIFE OF HER IN WHICH GARDEN THE SUMMER HOUSE HAD BELONGED.

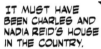

IT MUST HAVE BEEN CHARLES AND NADIA REID'S HOUSE IN THE COUNTRY.

WHICH MEANS IT WAS BEFORE NADIA RAN AWAY WITH THAT SCOTTISH ARTIST AND CHARLES TOOK ME WITH HIM TO SPAIN.

SPAIN SEEMED SO EXOTIC AND DANGEROUS IN THOSE DAYS.

YOU ASKED ME TO MARRY YOU.

WHY DID I SAY NO?

YOU WERE A PLEASANT-ENOUGH YOUNG MAN.

HE TOOK WHAT WAS LEFT OF HER VIRGINITY ON A SPANISH BEACH, ON A WARM SUMMER NIGHT.

I WAS TWENTY YEARS OLD AND THOUGHT MYSELF SO OLD.

HER FIRST THOUGHT IS HOW YOUNG THE GIRL LOOKS.

14

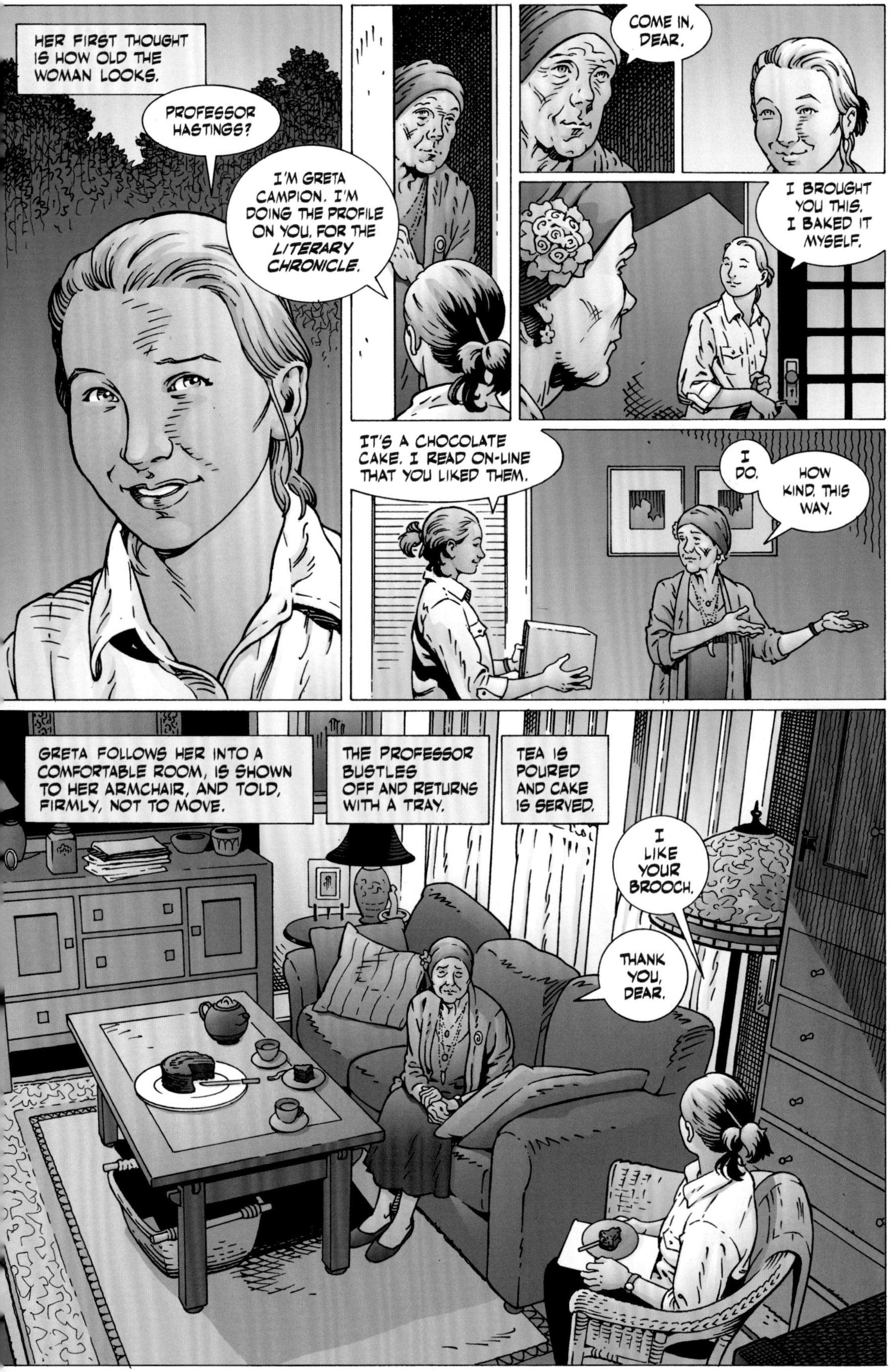
HER FIRST THOUGHT IS HOW OLD THE WOMAN LOOKS.
PROFESSOR HASTINGS?
I'M GRETA CAMPION. I'M DOING THE PROFILE ON YOU, FOR THE *LITERARY CHRONICLE*.
COME IN, DEAR.
I BROUGHT YOU THIS. I BAKED IT MYSELF.
IT'S A CHOCOLATE CAKE. I READ ON-LINE THAT YOU LIKED THEM.
I DO.
HOW KIND. THIS WAY.
GRETA FOLLOWS HER INTO A COMFORTABLE ROOM, IS SHOWN TO HER ARMCHAIR, AND TOLD, FIRMLY, NOT TO MOVE.
THE PROFESSOR BUSTLES OFF AND RETURNS WITH A TRAY.
TEA IS POURED AND CAKE IS SERVED.
I LIKE YOUR BROOCH.
THANK YOU, DEAR.

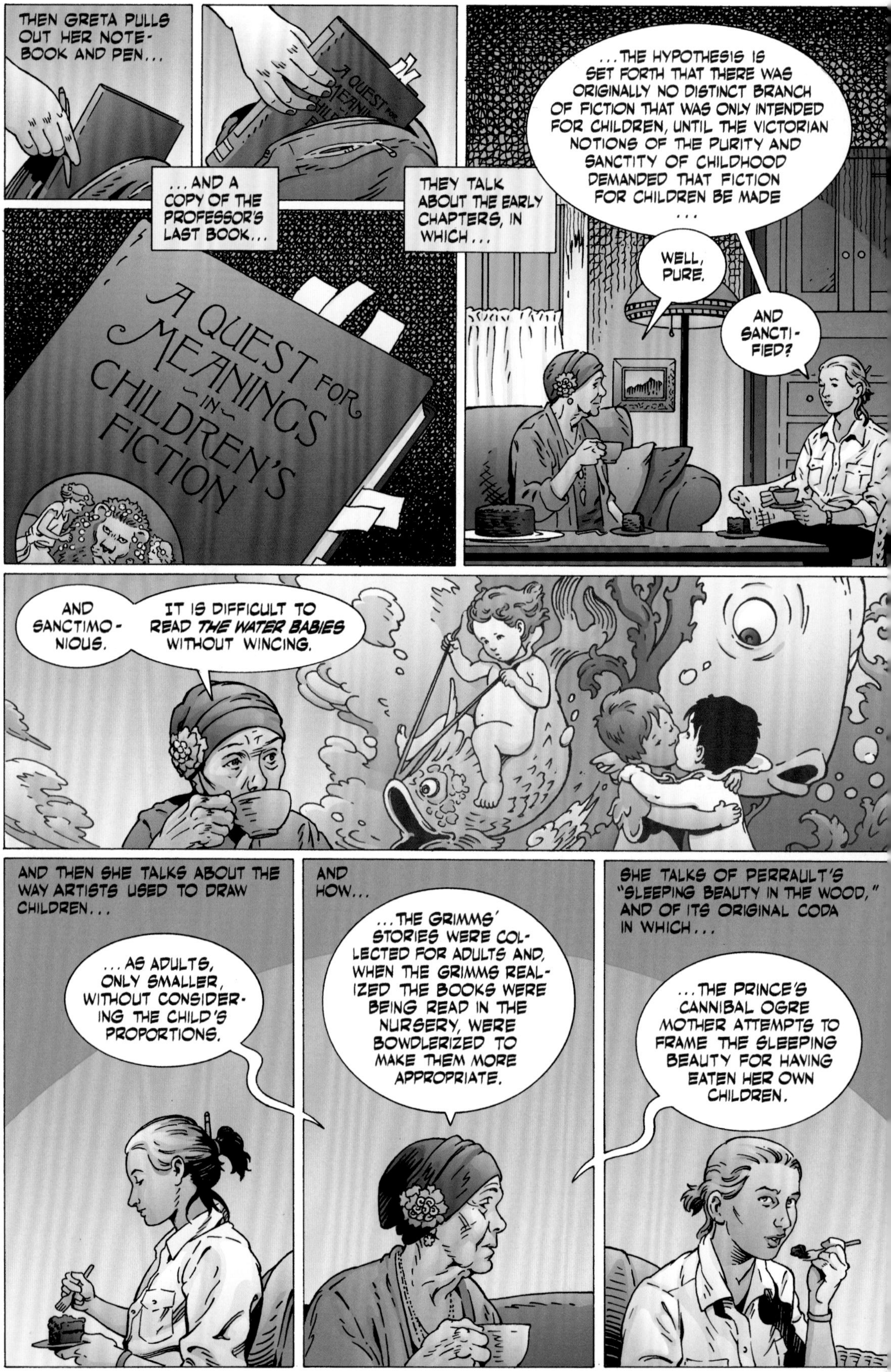
THEN GRETA PULLS OUT HER NOTE-BOOK AND PEN...
...AND A COPY OF THE PROFESSOR'S LAST BOOK...
A QUEST FOR MEANINGS IN CHILDREN'S FICTION
THEY TALK ABOUT THE EARLY CHAPTERS, IN WHICH...
...THE HYPOTHESIS IS SET FORTH THAT THERE WAS ORIGINALLY NO DISTINCT BRANCH OF FICTION THAT WAS ONLY INTENDED FOR CHILDREN, UNTIL THE VICTORIAN NOTIONS OF THE PURITY AND SANCTITY OF CHILDHOOD DEMANDED THAT FICTION FOR CHILDREN BE MADE...
WELL, PURE.
AND SANCTI-FIED?
AND SANCTIMO-NIOUS.
IT IS DIFFICULT TO READ *THE WATER BABIES* WITHOUT WINCING.
AND THEN SHE TALKS ABOUT THE WAY ARTISTS USED TO DRAW CHILDREN...
...AS ADULTS, ONLY SMALLER, WITHOUT CONSIDER-ING THE CHILD'S PROPORTIONS.
AND HOW...
...THE GRIMMS' STORIES WERE COL-LECTED FOR ADULTS AND, WHEN THE GRIMMS REAL-IZED THE BOOKS WERE BEING READ IN THE NURSERY, WERE BOWDLERIZED TO MAKE THEM MORE APPROPRIATE.
SHE TALKS OF PERRAULT'S "SLEEPING BEAUTY IN THE WOOD," AND OF ITS ORIGINAL CODA IN WHICH...
...THE PRINCE'S CANNIBAL OGRE MOTHER ATTEMPTS TO FRAME THE SLEEPING BEAUTY FOR HAVING EATEN HER OWN CHILDREN.

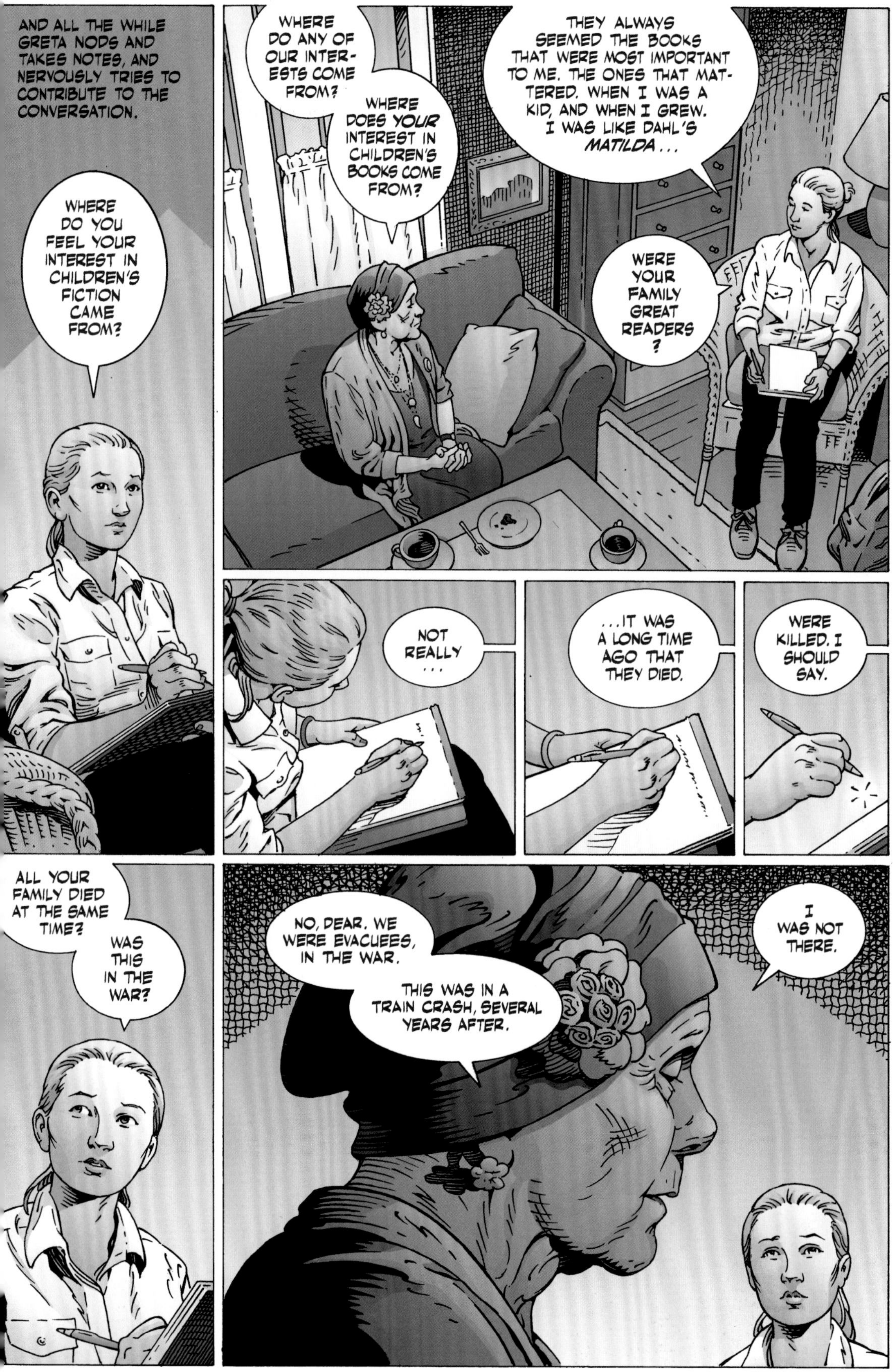
AND ALL THE WHILE GRETA NODS AND TAKES NOTES, AND NERVOUSLY TRIES TO CONTRIBUTE TO THE CONVERSATION.
WHERE DO YOU FEEL YOUR INTEREST IN CHILDREN'S FICTION CAME FROM?
WHERE DO ANY OF OUR INTER-ESTS COME FROM?
WHERE DOES *YOUR* INTEREST IN CHILDREN'S BOOKS COME FROM?
THEY ALWAYS SEEMED THE BOOKS THAT WERE MOST IMPORTANT TO ME. THE ONES THAT MAT-TERED. WHEN I WAS A KID, AND WHEN I GREW. I WAS LIKE DAHL'S *MATILDA* . . .
WERE YOUR FAMILY GREAT READERS ?
NOT REALLY . . .
. . .IT WAS A LONG TIME AGO THAT THEY DIED.
WERE KILLED, I SHOULD SAY.
ALL YOUR FAMILY DIED AT THE SAME TIME?
WAS THIS IN THE WAR?
NO, DEAR. WE WERE EVACUEES, IN THE WAR.
THIS WAS IN A TRAIN CRASH, SEVERAL YEARS AFTER.
I WAS NOT THERE.

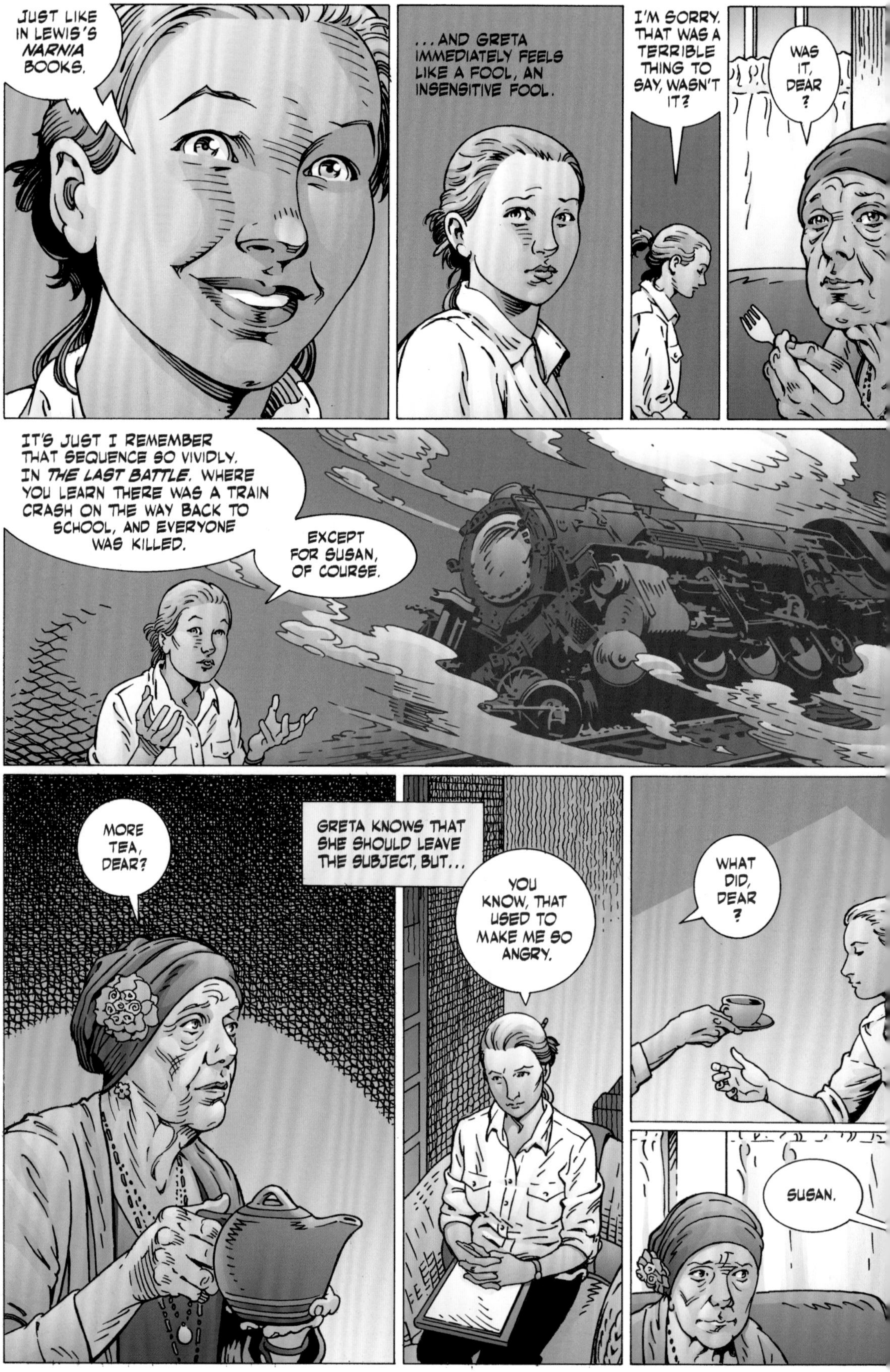
JUST LIKE IN LEWIS'S *NARNIA* BOOKS.
...AND GRETA IMMEDIATELY FEELS LIKE A FOOL, AN INSENSITIVE FOOL.
I'M SORRY. THAT WAS A TERRIBLE THING TO SAY, WASN'T IT?
WAS IT, DEAR?
IT'S JUST I REMEMBER THAT SEQUENCE SO VIVIDLY. IN *THE LAST BATTLE*. WHERE YOU LEARN THERE WAS A TRAIN CRASH ON THE WAY BACK TO SCHOOL, AND EVERYONE WAS KILLED.
EXCEPT FOR SUSAN, OF COURSE.
MORE TEA, DEAR?
GRETA KNOWS THAT SHE SHOULD LEAVE THE SUBJECT, BUT...
YOU KNOW, THAT USED TO MAKE ME SO ANGRY.
WHAT DID, DEAR?
SUSAN.

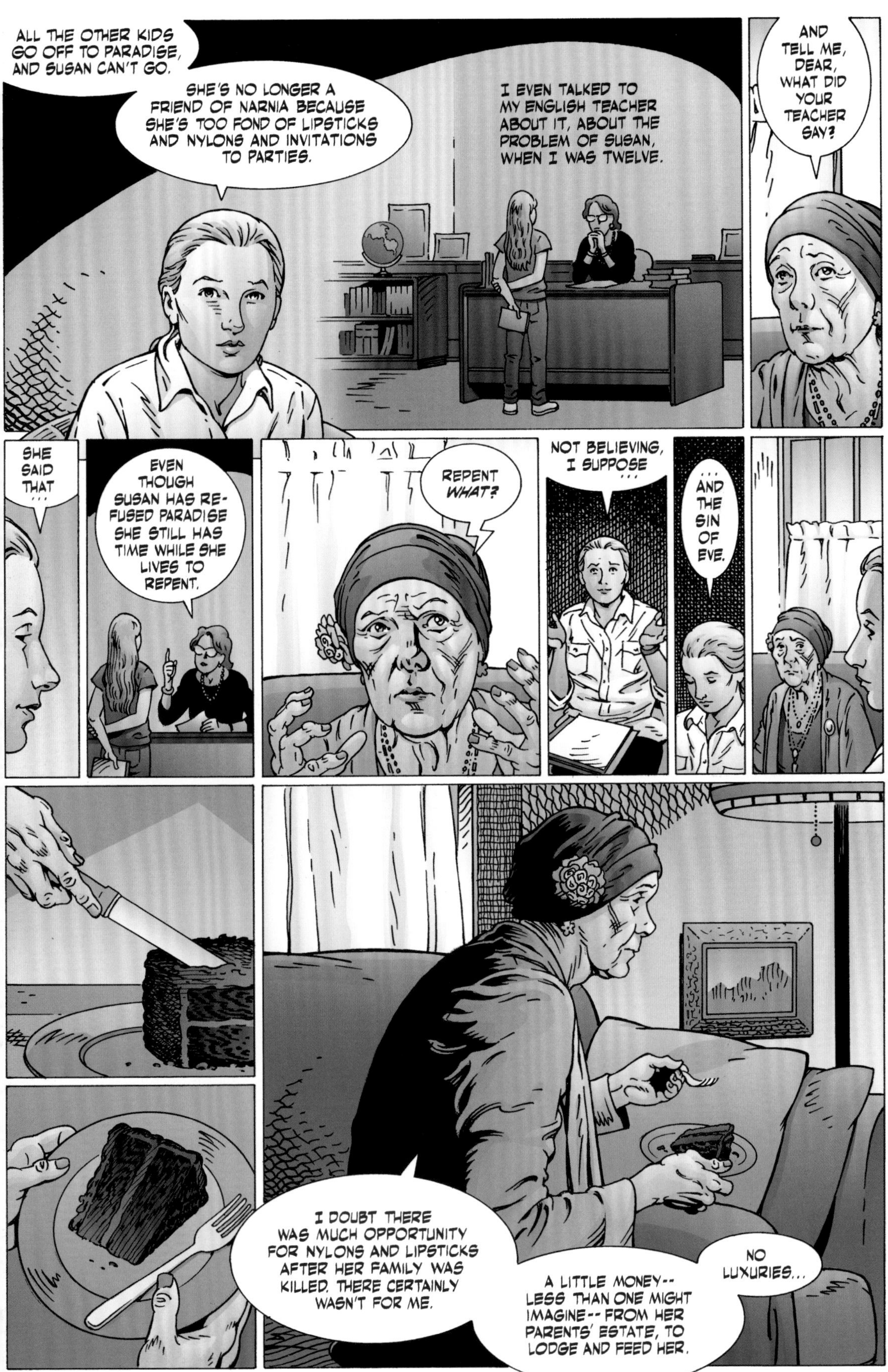
ALL THE OTHER KIDS GO OFF TO PARADISE, AND SUSAN CAN'T GO.
SHE'S NO LONGER A FRIEND OF NARNIA BECAUSE SHE'S TOO FOND OF LIPSTICKS AND NYLONS AND INVITATIONS TO PARTIES.
I EVEN TALKED TO MY ENGLISH TEACHER ABOUT IT, ABOUT THE PROBLEM OF SUSAN, WHEN I WAS TWELVE.
AND TELL ME, DEAR, WHAT DID YOUR TEACHER SAY?
SHE SAID THAT . . .
EVEN THOUGH SUSAN HAS RE-FUSED PARADISE SHE STILL HAS TIME WHILE SHE LIVES TO REPENT.
REPENT *WHAT?*
NOT BELIEVING, I SUPPOSE . . .
. . . AND THE SIN OF EVE.
I DOUBT THERE WAS MUCH OPPORTUNITY FOR NYLONS AND LIPSTICKS AFTER HER FAMILY WAS KILLED. THERE CERTAINLY WASN'T FOR ME.
NO LUXURIES...
A LITTLE MONEY-- LESS THAN ONE MIGHT IMAGINE-- FROM HER PARENTS' ESTATE, TO LODGE AND FEED HER.

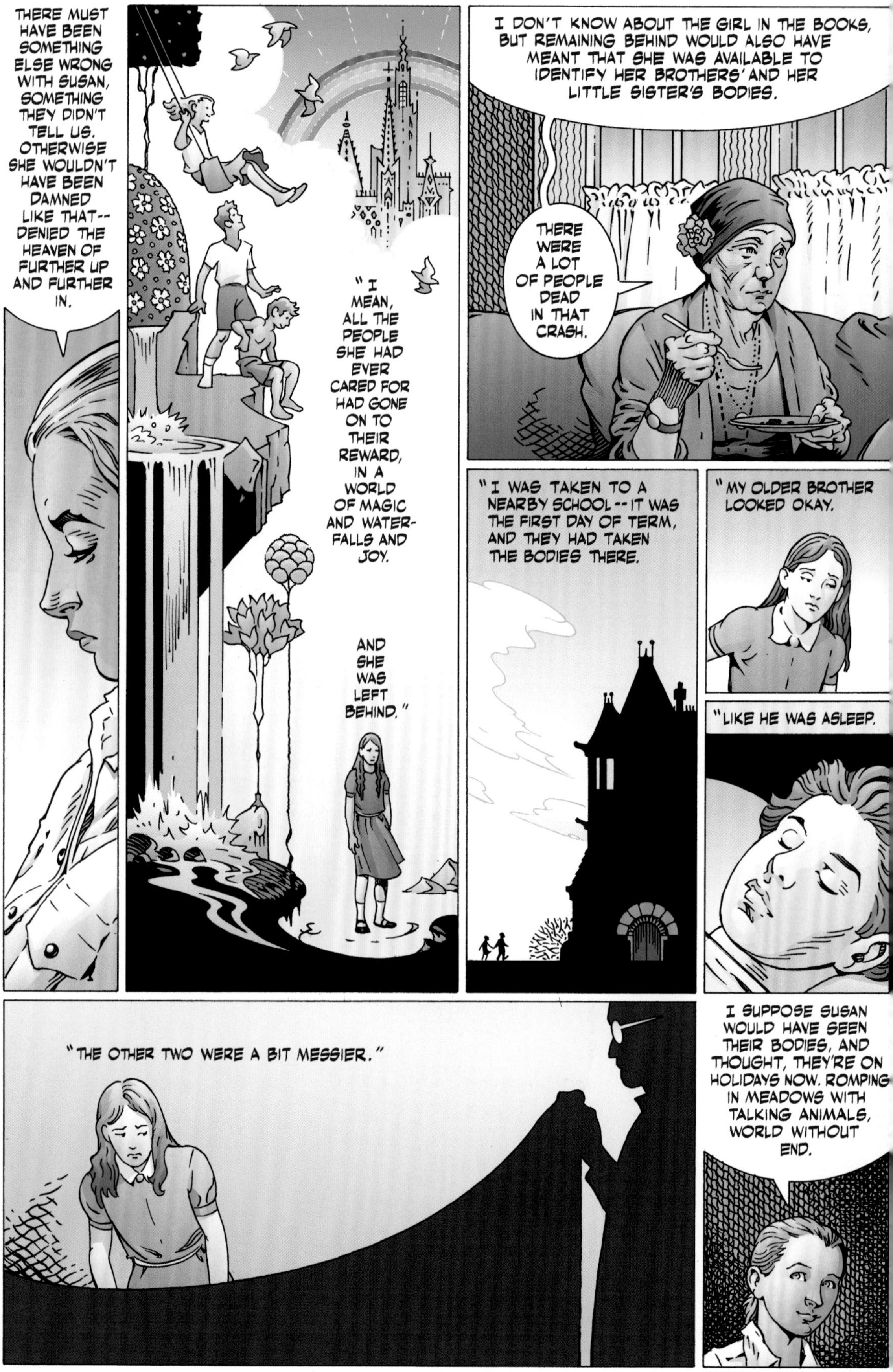
THERE MUST HAVE BEEN SOMETHING ELSE WRONG WITH SUSAN, SOMETHING THEY DIDN'T TELL US. OTHERWISE SHE WOULDN'T HAVE BEEN DAMNED LIKE THAT-- DENIED THE HEAVEN OF FURTHER UP AND FURTHER IN.
"I MEAN, ALL THE PEOPLE SHE HAD EVER CARED FOR HAD GONE ON TO THEIR REWARD, IN A WORLD OF MAGIC AND WATER-FALLS AND JOY.
AND SHE WAS LEFT BEHIND."
I DON'T KNOW ABOUT THE GIRL IN THE BOOKS, BUT REMAINING BEHIND WOULD ALSO HAVE MEANT THAT SHE WAS AVAILABLE TO IDENTIFY HER BROTHERS' AND HER LITTLE SISTER'S BODIES.
THERE WERE A LOT OF PEOPLE DEAD IN THAT CRASH.
"I WAS TAKEN TO A NEARBY SCHOOL -- IT WAS THE FIRST DAY OF TERM, AND THEY HAD TAKEN THE BODIES THERE.
"MY OLDER BROTHER LOOKED OKAY.
"LIKE HE WAS ASLEEP.
"THE OTHER TWO WERE A BIT MESSIER."
I SUPPOSE SUSAN WOULD HAVE SEEN THEIR BODIES, AND THOUGHT, THEY'RE ON HOLIDAYS NOW. ROMPING IN MEADOWS WITH TALKING ANIMALS, WORLD WITHOUT END.

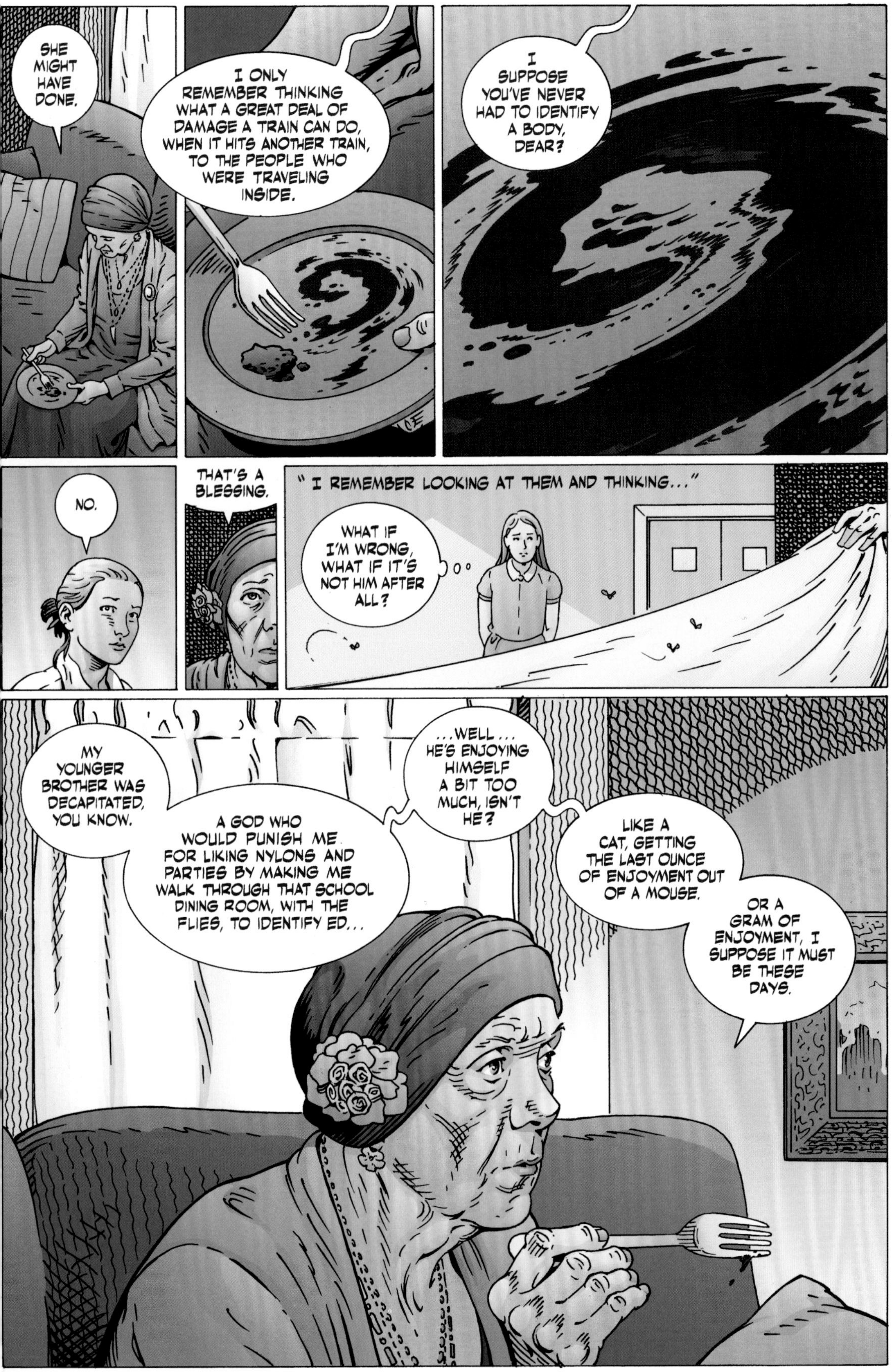
SHE MIGHT HAVE DONE.
I ONLY REMEMBER THINKING WHAT A GREAT DEAL OF DAMAGE A TRAIN CAN DO, WHEN IT HITS ANOTHER TRAIN, TO THE PEOPLE WHO WERE TRAVELING INSIDE.
I SUPPOSE YOU'VE NEVER HAD TO IDENTIFY A BODY, DEAR?
NO.
THAT'S A BLESSING.
" I REMEMBER LOOKING AT THEM AND THINKING..."
WHAT IF I'M WRONG, WHAT IF IT'S NOT HIM AFTER ALL?
MY YOUNGER BROTHER WAS DECAPITATED, YOU KNOW.
A GOD WHO WOULD PUNISH ME FOR LIKING NYLONS AND PARTIES BY MAKING ME WALK THROUGH THAT SCHOOL DINING ROOM, WITH THE FLIES, TO IDENTIFY ED...
...WELL... HE'S ENJOYING HIMSELF A BIT TOO MUCH, ISN'T HE?
LIKE A CAT, GETTING THE LAST OUNCE OF ENJOYMENT OUT OF A MOUSE.
OR A GRAM OF ENJOYMENT, I SUPPOSE IT MUST BE THESE DAYS.

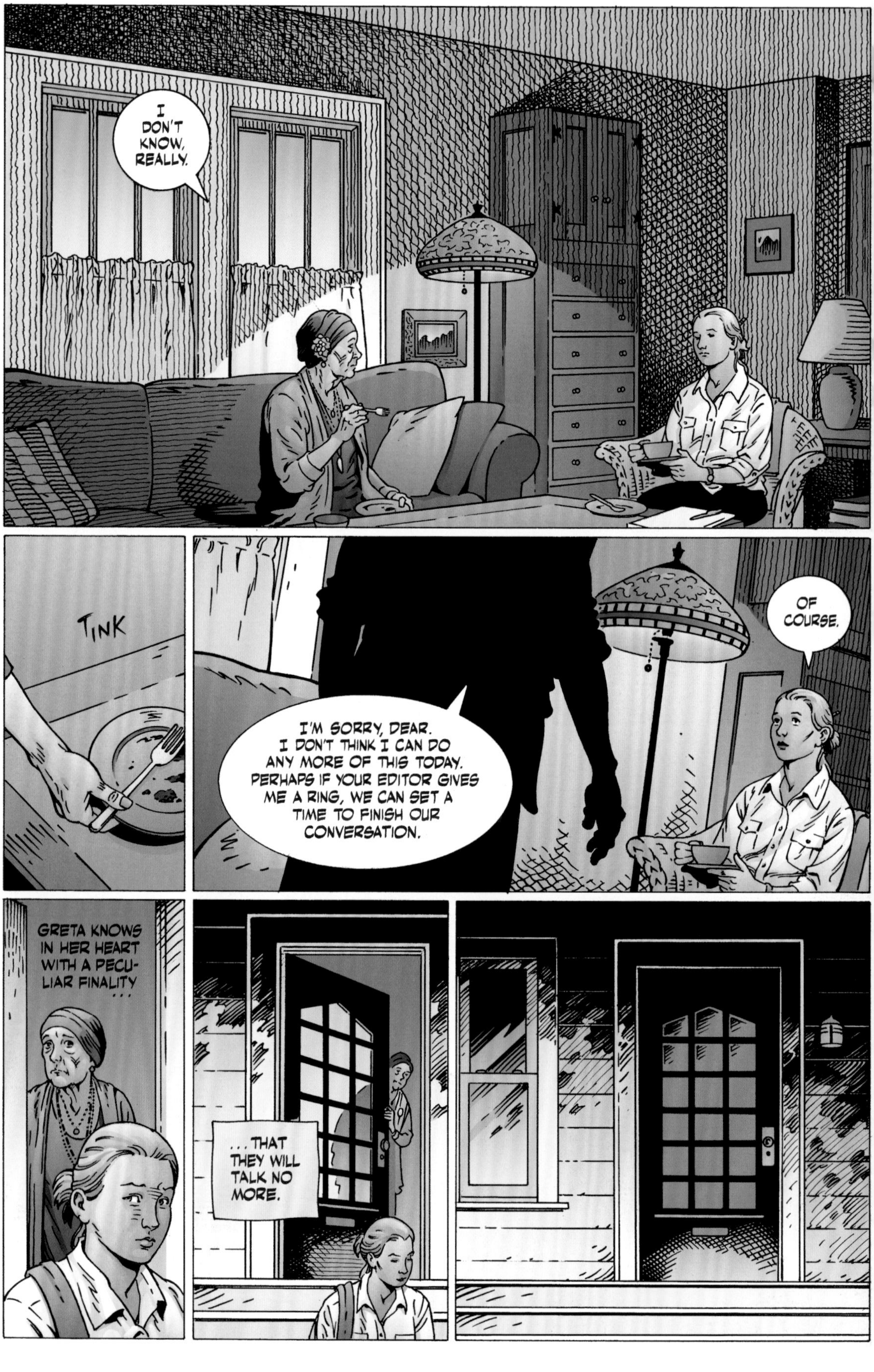
I DON'T KNOW, REALLY.
TINK
I'M SORRY, DEAR. I DON'T THINK I CAN DO ANY MORE OF THIS TODAY. PERHAPS IF YOUR EDITOR GIVES ME A RING, WE CAN SET A TIME TO FINISH OUR CONVERSATION.
OF COURSE.
GRETA KNOWS IN HER HEART WITH A PECULIAR FINALITY . . .
. . . THAT THEY WILL TALK NO MORE.

THAT NIGHT, THE PROFESSOR CLIMBS THE STAIRS OF HER HOUSE, SLOWLY, PAINSTAKINGLY, FLOOR BY FLOOR.

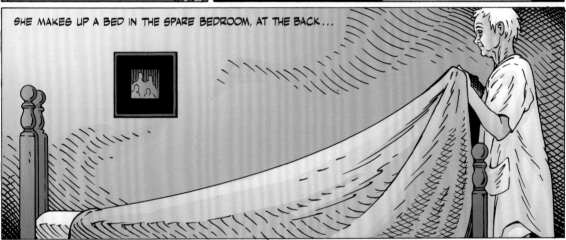

SHE MAKES UP A BED IN THE SPARE BEDROOM, AT THE BACK...

SHE PLACES A VASE ON THE DRESSING TABLE, CONTAINING PURPLE RHODODENDRON FLOWERS, STICKY AND VULGAR...

...TAKES FROM A BOX IN THE WARDROBE A PLASTIC SHOPPING BAG CONTAINING FOUR OLD PHOTOGRAPHIC ALBUMS...

...AND CLIMBS INTO THE BED THAT WAS HERS AS A CHILD.

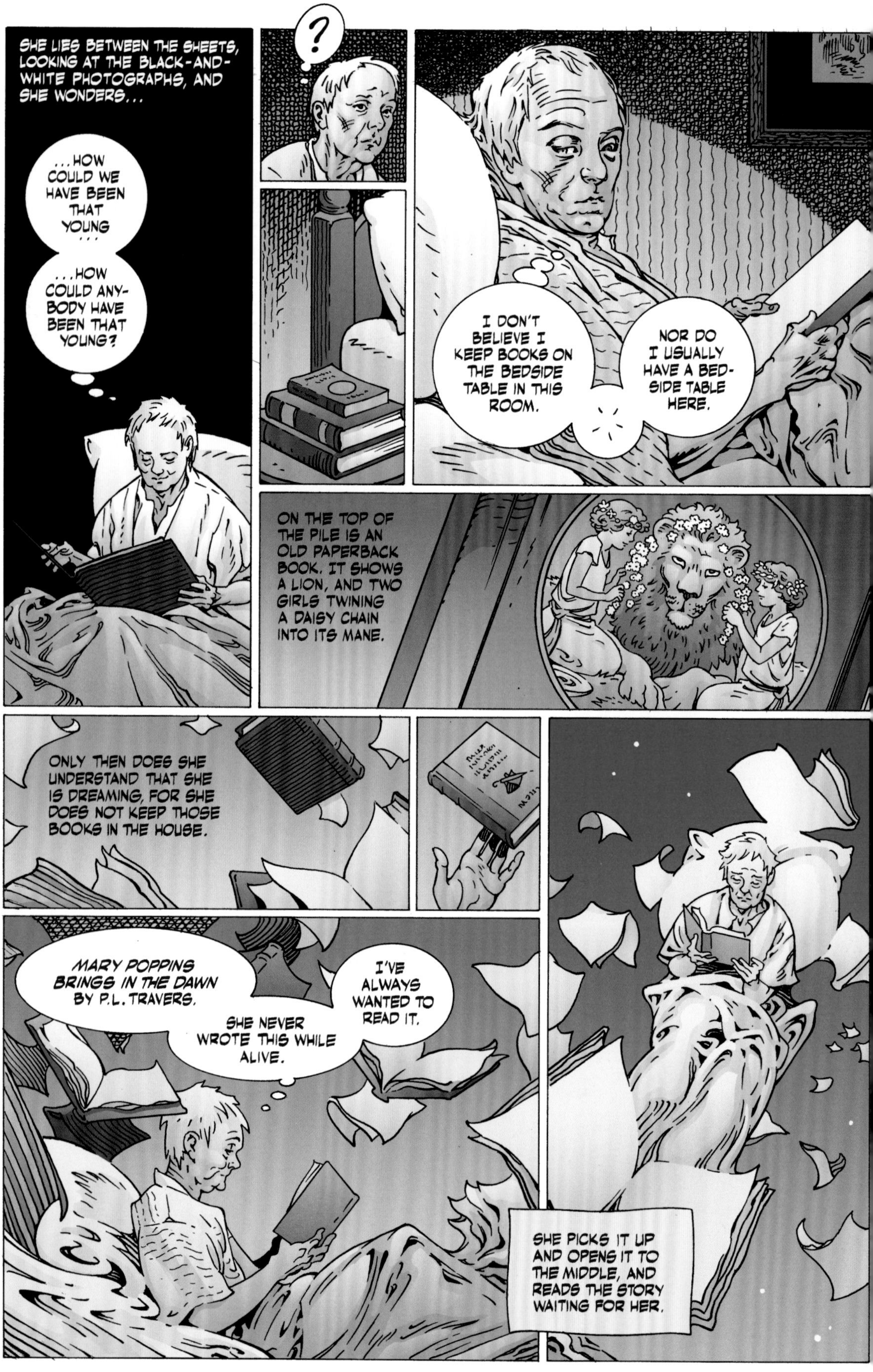
SHE LIES BETWEEN THE SHEETS, LOOKING AT THE BLACK-AND-WHITE PHOTOGRAPHS, AND SHE WONDERS...
...HOW COULD WE HAVE BEEN THAT YOUNG...
...HOW COULD ANYBODY HAVE BEEN THAT YOUNG?
?
I DON'T BELIEVE I KEEP BOOKS ON THE BEDSIDE TABLE IN THIS ROOM.
NOR DO I USUALLY HAVE A BEDSIDE TABLE HERE.
ON THE TOP OF THE PILE IS AN OLD PAPERBACK BOOK. IT SHOWS A LION, AND TWO GIRLS TWINING A DAISY CHAIN INTO ITS MANE.
ONLY THEN DOES SHE UNDERSTAND THAT SHE IS DREAMING, FOR SHE DOES NOT KEEP THOSE BOOKS IN THE HOUSE.
MARY POPPINS BRINGS IN THE DAWN BY P.L. TRAVERS.
I'VE ALWAYS WANTED TO READ IT.
SHE NEVER WROTE THIS WHILE ALIVE.
SHE PICKS IT UP AND OPENS IT TO THE MIDDLE, AND READS THE STORY WAITING FOR HER.

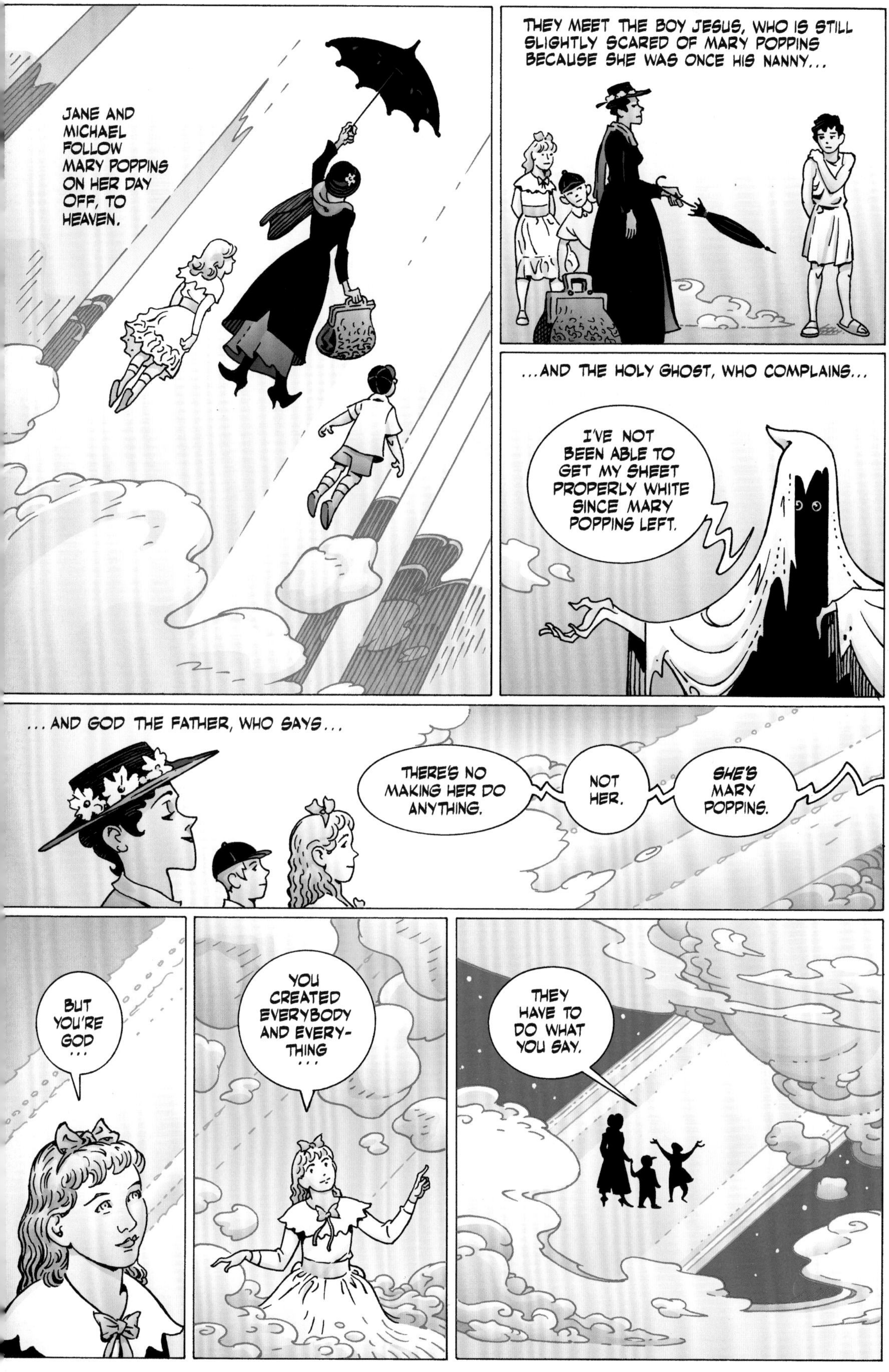
JANE AND MICHAEL FOLLOW MARY POPPINS ON HER DAY OFF, TO HEAVEN.
THEY MEET THE BOY JESUS, WHO IS STILL SLIGHTLY SCARED OF MARY POPPINS BECAUSE SHE WAS ONCE HIS NANNY...
...AND THE HOLY GHOST, WHO COMPLAINS...
I'VE NOT BEEN ABLE TO GET MY SHEET PROPERLY WHITE SINCE MARY POPPINS LEFT.
...AND GOD THE FATHER, WHO SAYS...
THERE'S NO MAKING HER DO ANYTHING.
NOT HER.
SHE'S MARY POPPINS.
BUT YOU'RE GOD...
YOU CREATED EVERYBODY AND EVERY-THING...
THEY HAVE TO DO WHAT YOU SAY.

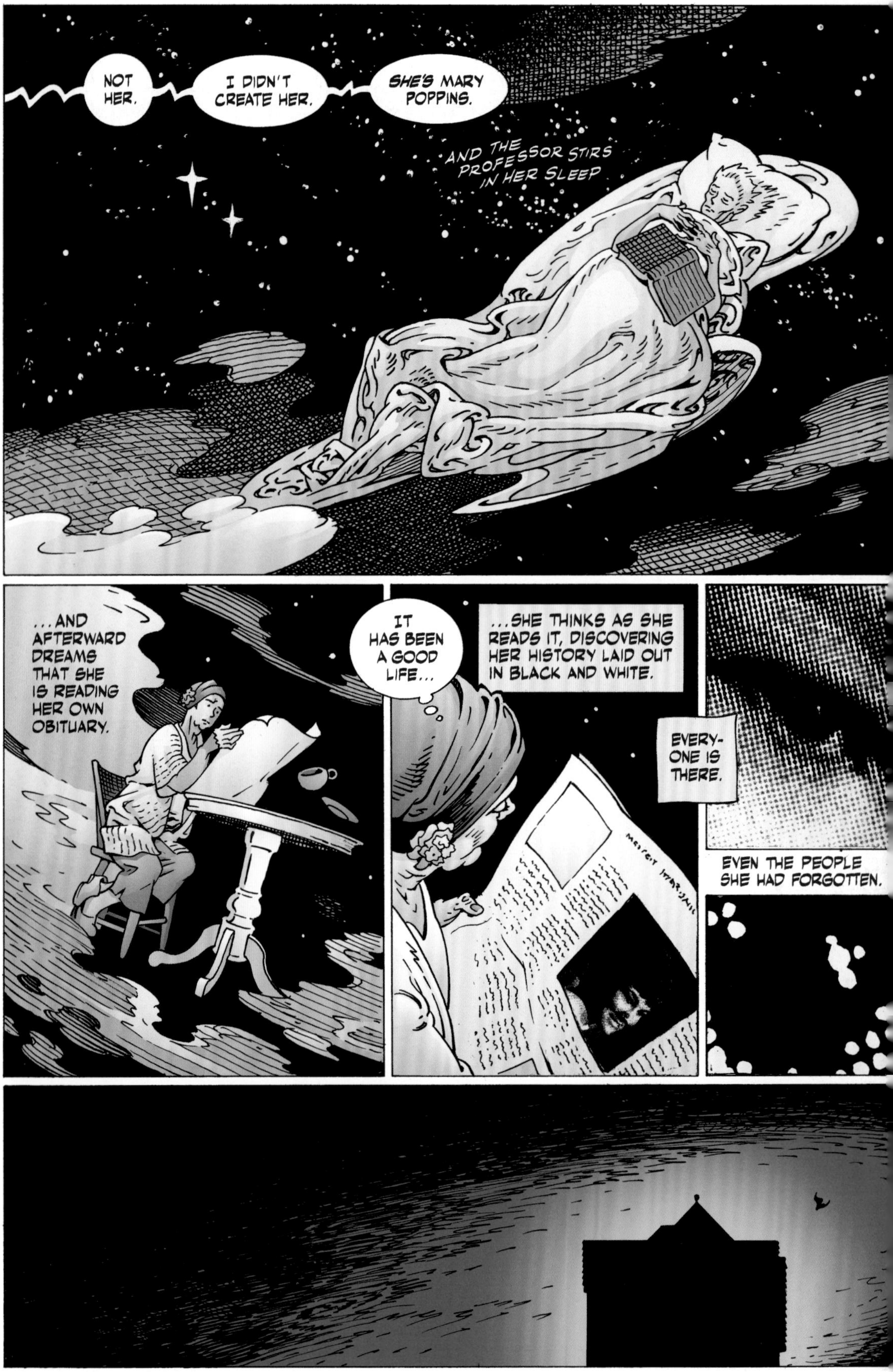
NOT HER.
I DIDN'T CREATE HER.
SHE'S MARY POPPINS.
AND THE PROFESSOR STIRS IN HER SLEEP
...AND AFTERWARD DREAMS THAT SHE IS READING HER OWN OBITUARY.
IT HAS BEEN A GOOD LIFE...
...SHE THINKS AS SHE READS IT, DISCOVERING HER HISTORY LAID OUT IN BLACK AND WHITE.
EVERY-ONE IS THERE.
EVEN THE PEOPLE SHE HAD FORGOTTEN.

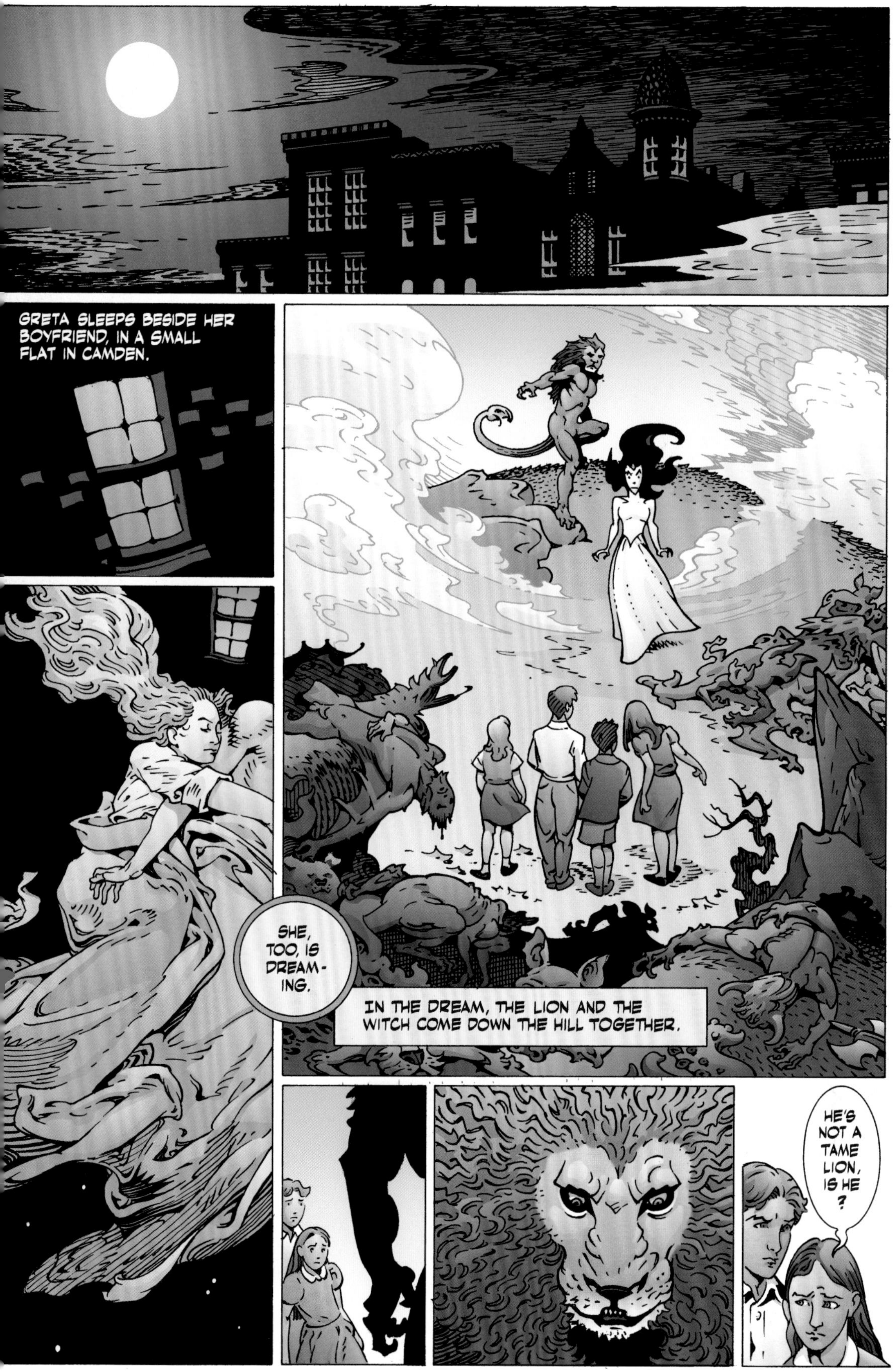
GRETA SLEEPS BESIDE HER BOYFRIEND, IN A SMALL FLAT IN CAMDEN.
SHE, TOO, IS DREAM-ING.
IN THE DREAM, THE LION AND THE WITCH COME DOWN THE HILL TOGETHER.
HE'S NOT A TAME LION, IS HE ?

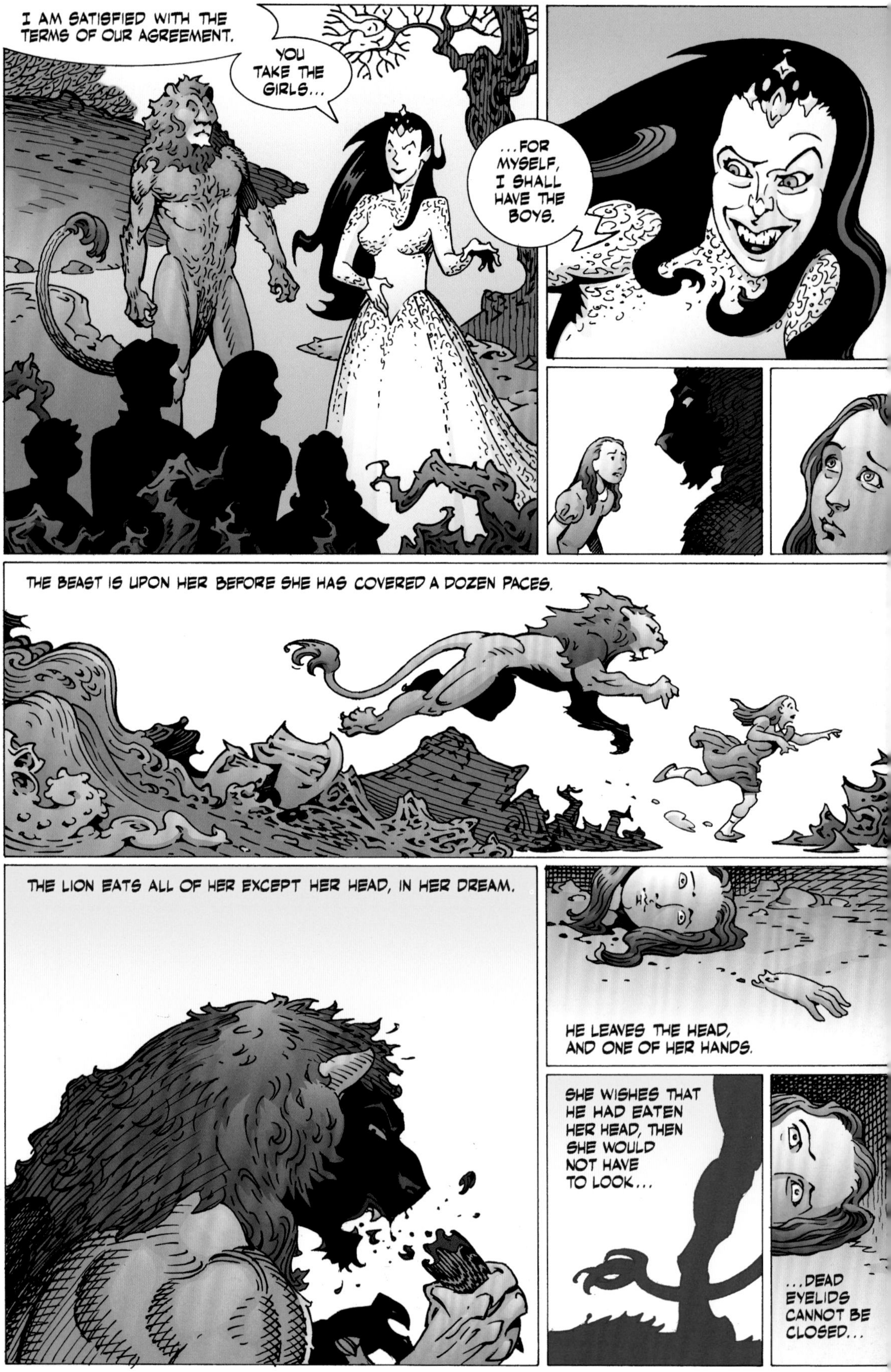
I AM SATISFIED WITH THE TERMS OF OUR AGREEMENT.
YOU TAKE THE GIRLS...
...FOR MYSELF, I SHALL HAVE THE BOYS.
THE BEAST IS UPON HER BEFORE SHE HAS COVERED A DOZEN PACES.
THE LION EATS ALL OF HER EXCEPT HER HEAD, IN HER DREAM.
HE LEAVES THE HEAD, AND ONE OF HER HANDS.
SHE WISHES THAT HE HAD EATEN HER HEAD, THEN SHE WOULD NOT HAVE TO LOOK...
...DEAD EYELIDS CANNOT BE CLOSED...

... AND SHE STARES, UNFLINCHING...

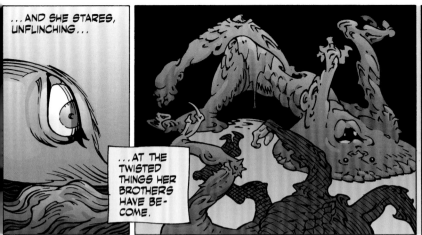

...AT THE TWISTED THINGS HER BROTHERS HAVE BECOME.

THE BEAST EATS HER LITTLE SISTER MORE SLOWLY, AND, IT SEEMS TO HER, WITH MORE RELISH THAN IT HAD EATEN HER.

BUT THEN...

...HER LITTLE SISTER HAD ALWAYS BEEN ITS FAVORITE.

NOW.

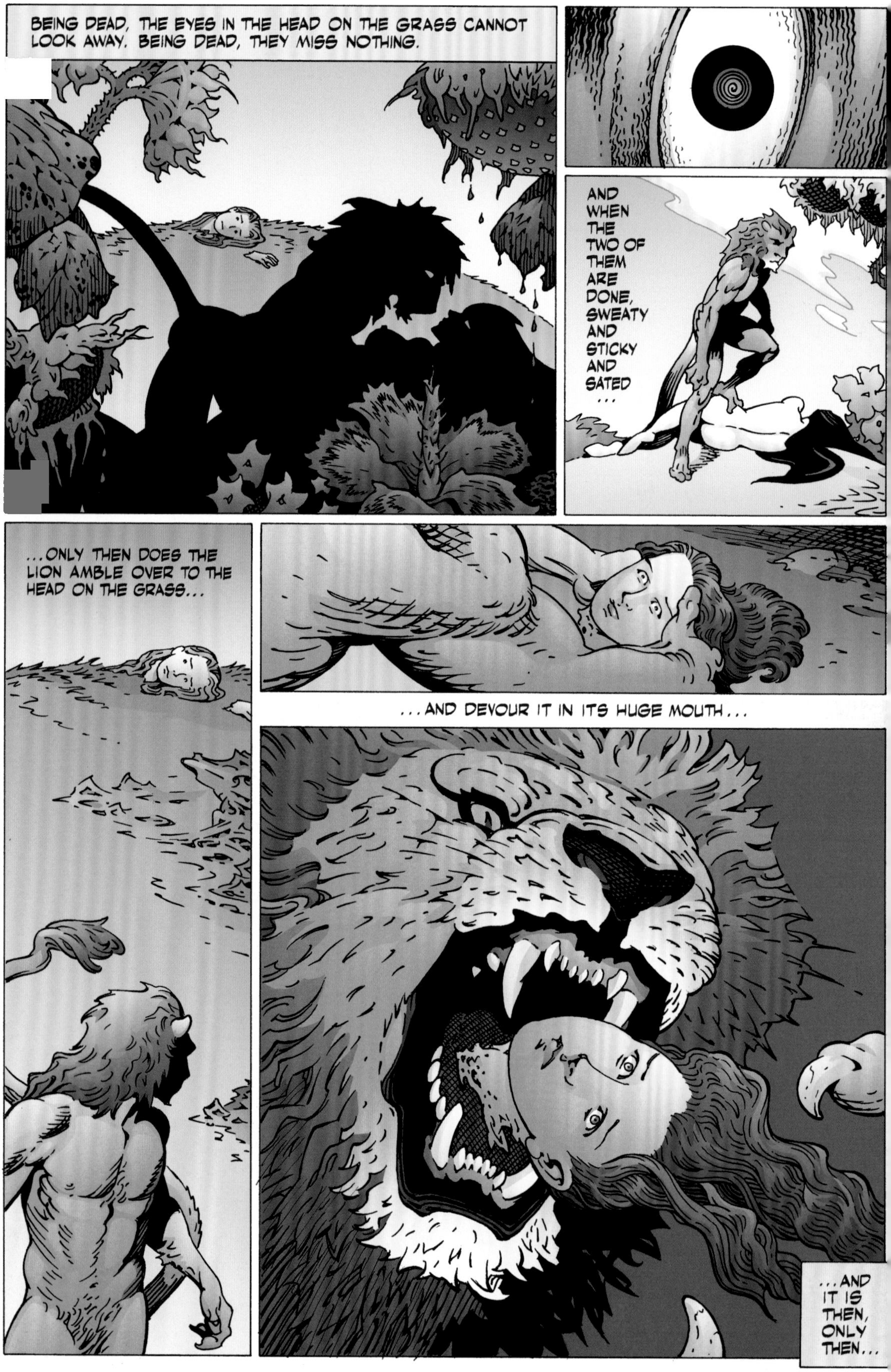
BEING DEAD, THE EYES IN THE HEAD ON THE GRASS CANNOT LOOK AWAY. BEING DEAD, THEY MISS NOTHING.
AND WHEN THE TWO OF THEM ARE DONE, SWEATY AND STICKY AND SATED ...
...ONLY THEN DOES THE LION AMBLE OVER TO THE HEAD ON THE GRASS...
...AND DEVOUR IT IN ITS HUGE MOUTH...
...AND IT IS THEN, ONLY THEN...

AHH H!

SHE TRIES TO WAKE HER BOY-FRIEND, BUT HE SNORES AND GRUNTS AND WILL NOT BE ROUSED.

IT'S TRUE.

SHE GREW UP.

SHE CARRIED ON.

SHE DIDN'T DIE.

SHE IMAGINES THE PRO-FESSOR, WAKING IN THE NIGHT AND LISTENING TO THE NOISES COMING FROM THE OLD WARDROBE IN THE CORNER...

...TO THE RUSTLINGS OF ALL THESE GLIDING GHOSTS, WHICH MIGHT BE MISTAKEN FOR THE SCURRIES OF MICE OR RATS, TO THE PADDING OF ENORMOUS VELVET PAWS...

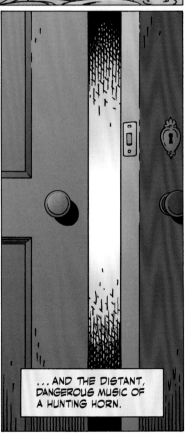

...AND THE DISTANT, DANGEROUS MUSIC OF A HUNTING HORN.

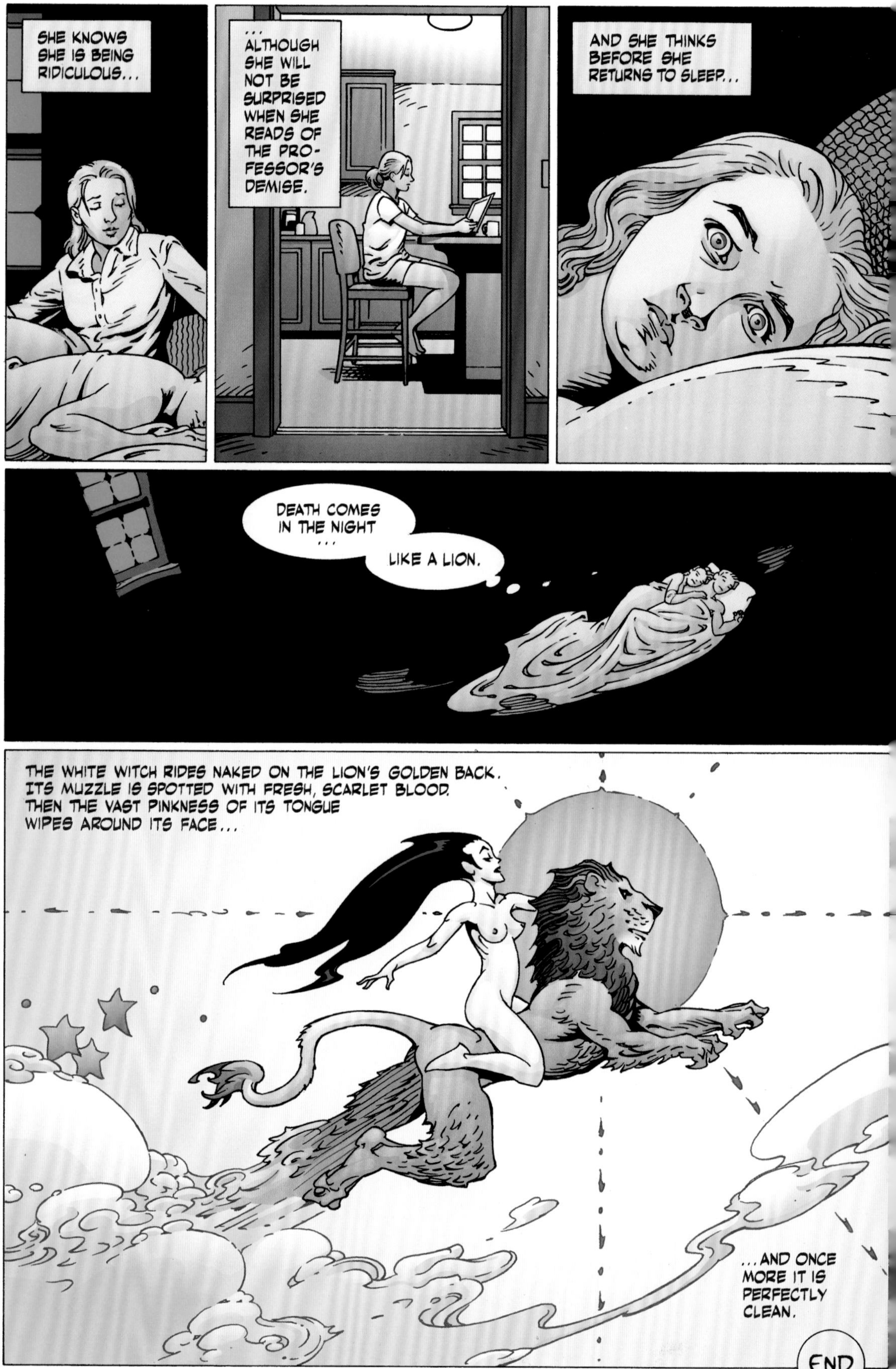
SHE KNOWS SHE IS BEING RIDICULOUS...
...ALTHOUGH SHE WILL NOT BE SURPRISED WHEN SHE READS OF THE PRO-FESSOR'S DEMISE.
AND SHE THINKS BEFORE SHE RETURNS TO SLEEP...
DEATH COMES IN THE NIGHT ...
LIKE A LION.
THE WHITE WITCH RIDES NAKED ON THE LION'S GOLDEN BACK. ITS MUZZLE IS SPOTTED WITH FRESH, SCARLET BLOOD. THEN THE VAST PINKNESS OF ITS TONGUE WIPES AROUND ITS FACE...
...AND ONCE MORE IT IS PERFECTLY CLEAN.
END

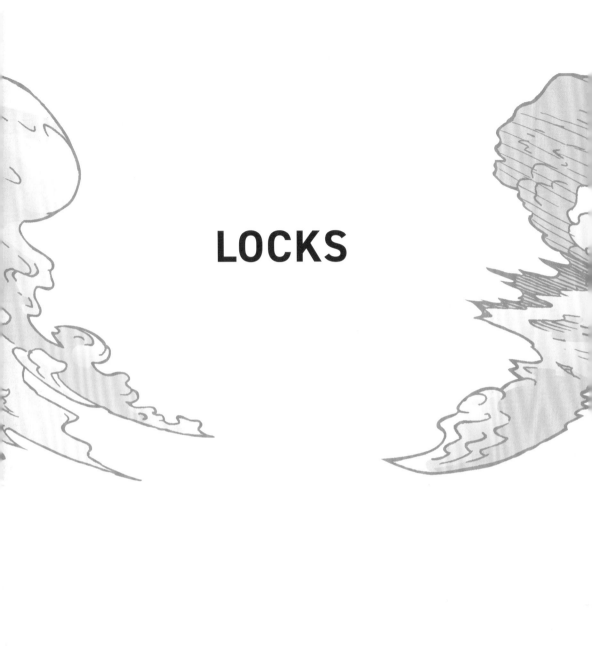

LOCKS

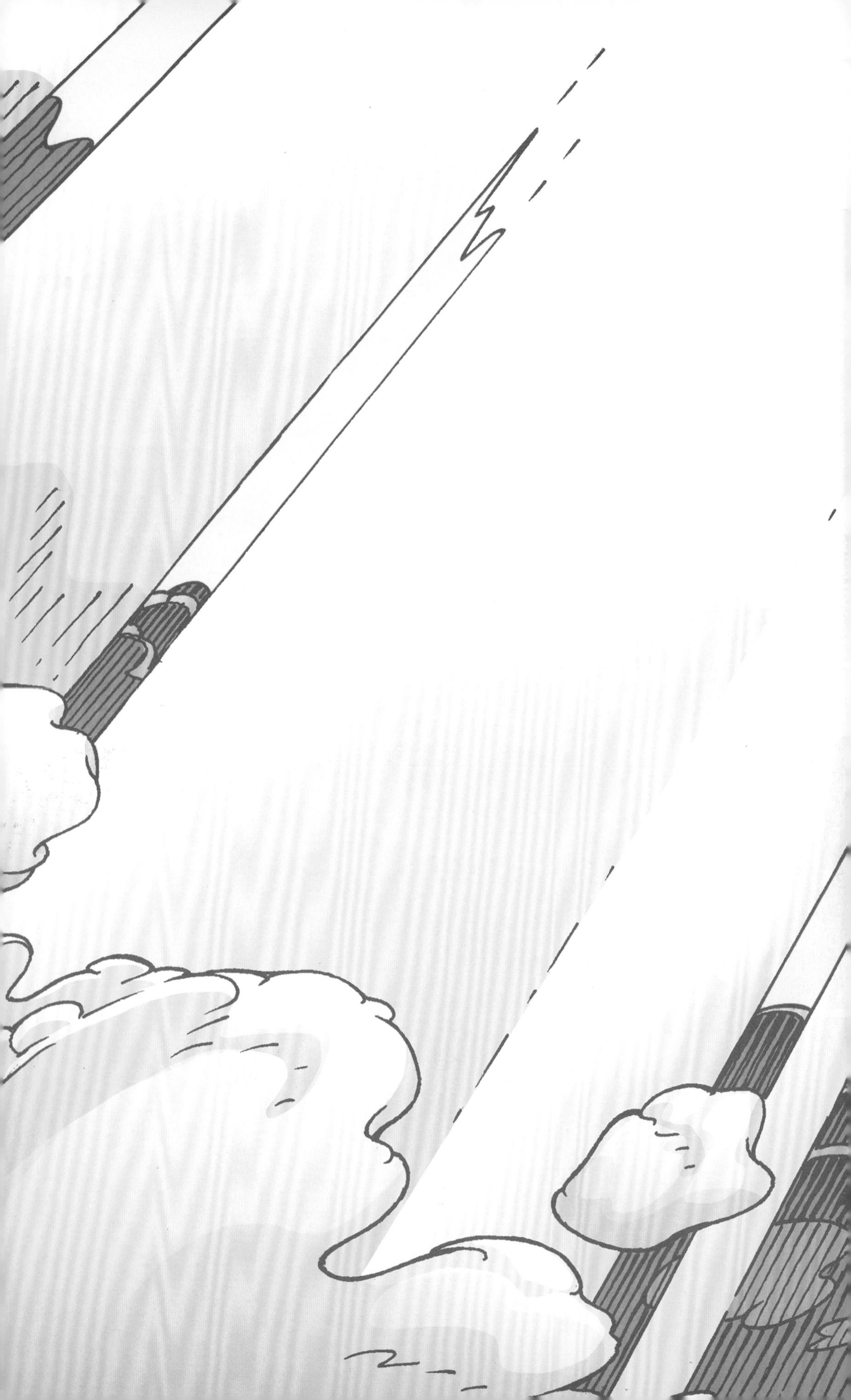

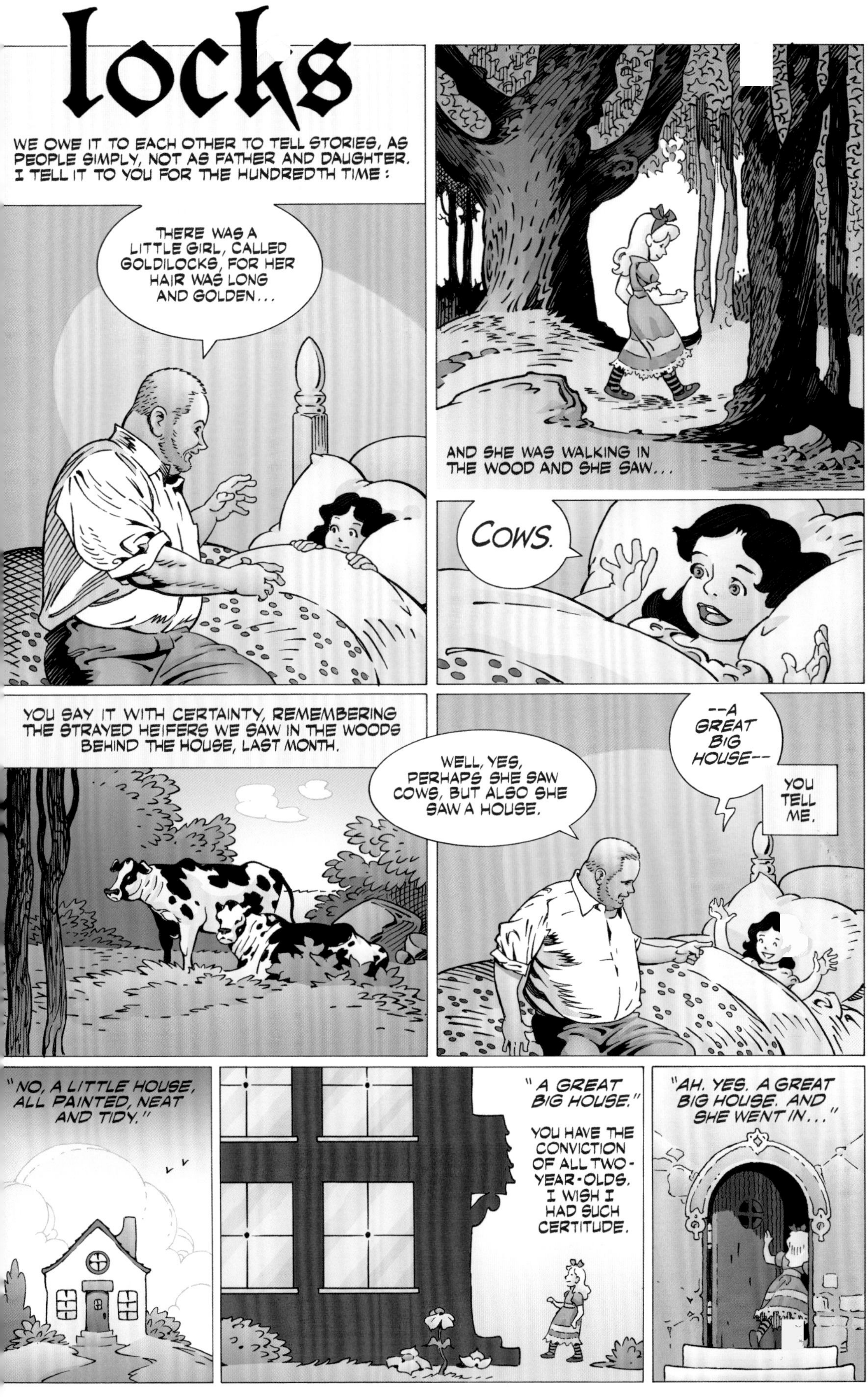
locks
WE OWE IT TO EACH OTHER TO TELL STORIES, AS PEOPLE SIMPLY, NOT AS FATHER AND DAUGHTER. I TELL IT TO YOU FOR THE HUNDREDTH TIME:
THERE WAS A LITTLE GIRL, CALLED GOLDILOCKS, FOR HER HAIR WAS LONG AND GOLDEN...
AND SHE WAS WALKING IN THE WOOD AND SHE SAW...
COWS.
YOU SAY IT WITH CERTAINTY, REMEMBERING THE STRAYED HEIFERS WE SAW IN THE WOODS BEHIND THE HOUSE, LAST MONTH.
WELL, YES, PERHAPS SHE SAW COWS, BUT ALSO SHE SAW A HOUSE.
--A GREAT BIG HOUSE--
YOU TELL ME.
"NO, A LITTLE HOUSE, ALL PAINTED, NEAT AND TIDY."
"A GREAT BIG HOUSE."
YOU HAVE THE CONVICTION OF ALL TWO-YEAR-OLDS. I WISH I HAD SUCH CERTITUDE.
"AH. YES. A GREAT BIG HOUSE. AND SHE WENT IN..."

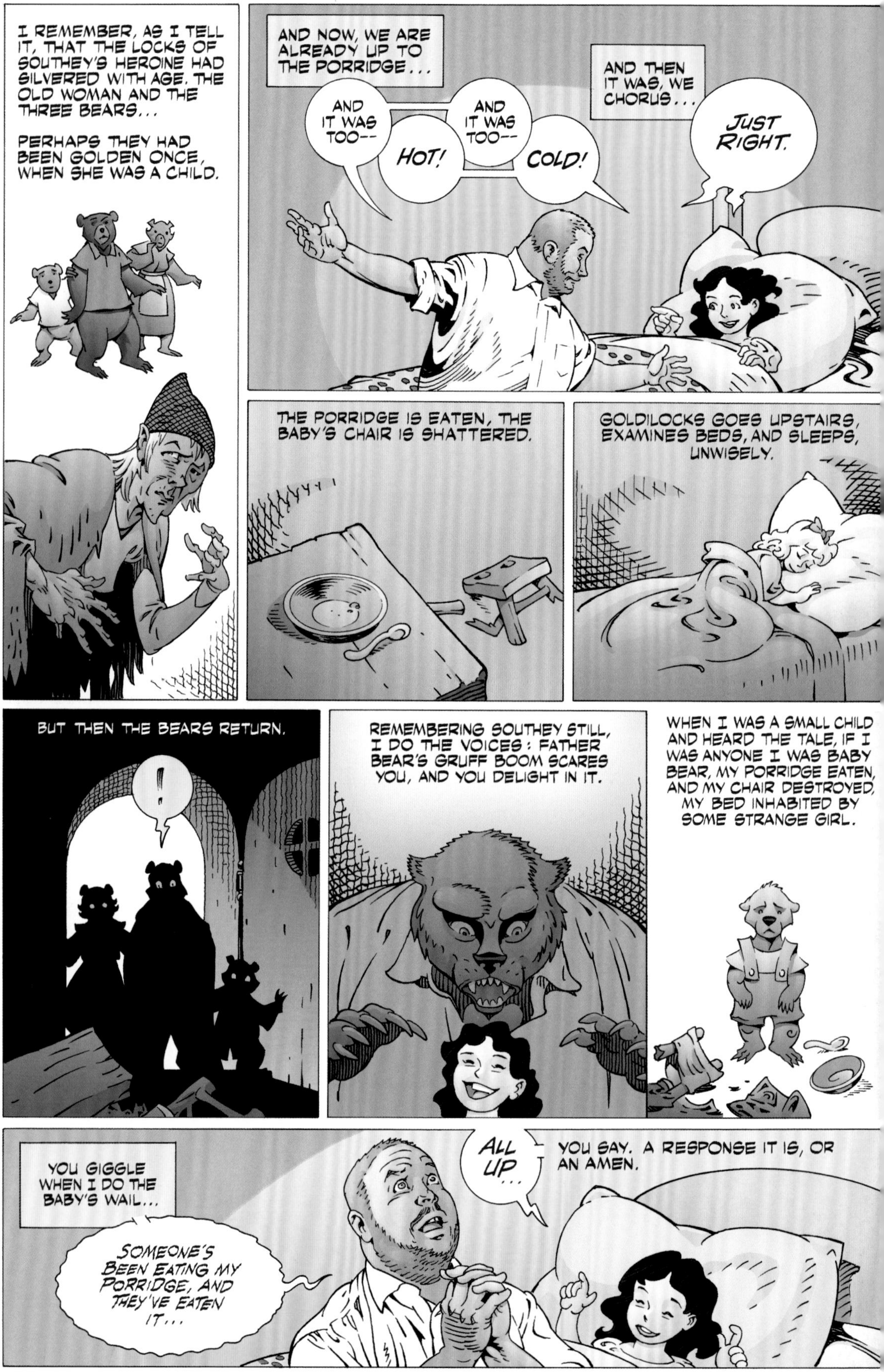
I REMEMBER, AS I TELL IT, THAT THE LOCKS OF SOUTHEY'S HEROINE HAD SILVERED WITH AGE. THE OLD WOMAN AND THE THREE BEARS...
PERHAPS THEY HAD BEEN GOLDEN ONCE, WHEN SHE WAS A CHILD.
AND NOW, WE ARE ALREADY UP TO THE PORRIDGE...
AND IT WAS TOO--
HOT!
AND IT WAS TOO--
COLD!
AND THEN IT WAS, WE CHORUS...
JUST RIGHT.
THE PORRIDGE IS EATEN, THE BABY'S CHAIR IS SHATTERED.
GOLDILOCKS GOES UPSTAIRS, EXAMINES BEDS, AND SLEEPS, UNWISELY.
BUT THEN THE BEARS RETURN.
!
REMEMBERING SOUTHEY STILL, I DO THE VOICES: FATHER BEAR'S GRUFF BOOM SCARES YOU, AND YOU DELIGHT IN IT.
WHEN I WAS A SMALL CHILD AND HEARD THE TALE, IF I WAS ANYONE I WAS BABY BEAR, MY PORRIDGE EATEN, AND MY CHAIR DESTROYED, MY BED INHABITED BY SOME STRANGE GIRL.
YOU GIGGLE WHEN I DO THE BABY'S WAIL...
SOMEONE'S BEEN EATING MY PORRIDGE, AND THEY'VE EATEN IT...
ALL UP...
YOU SAY. A RESPONSE IT IS, OR AN AMEN.

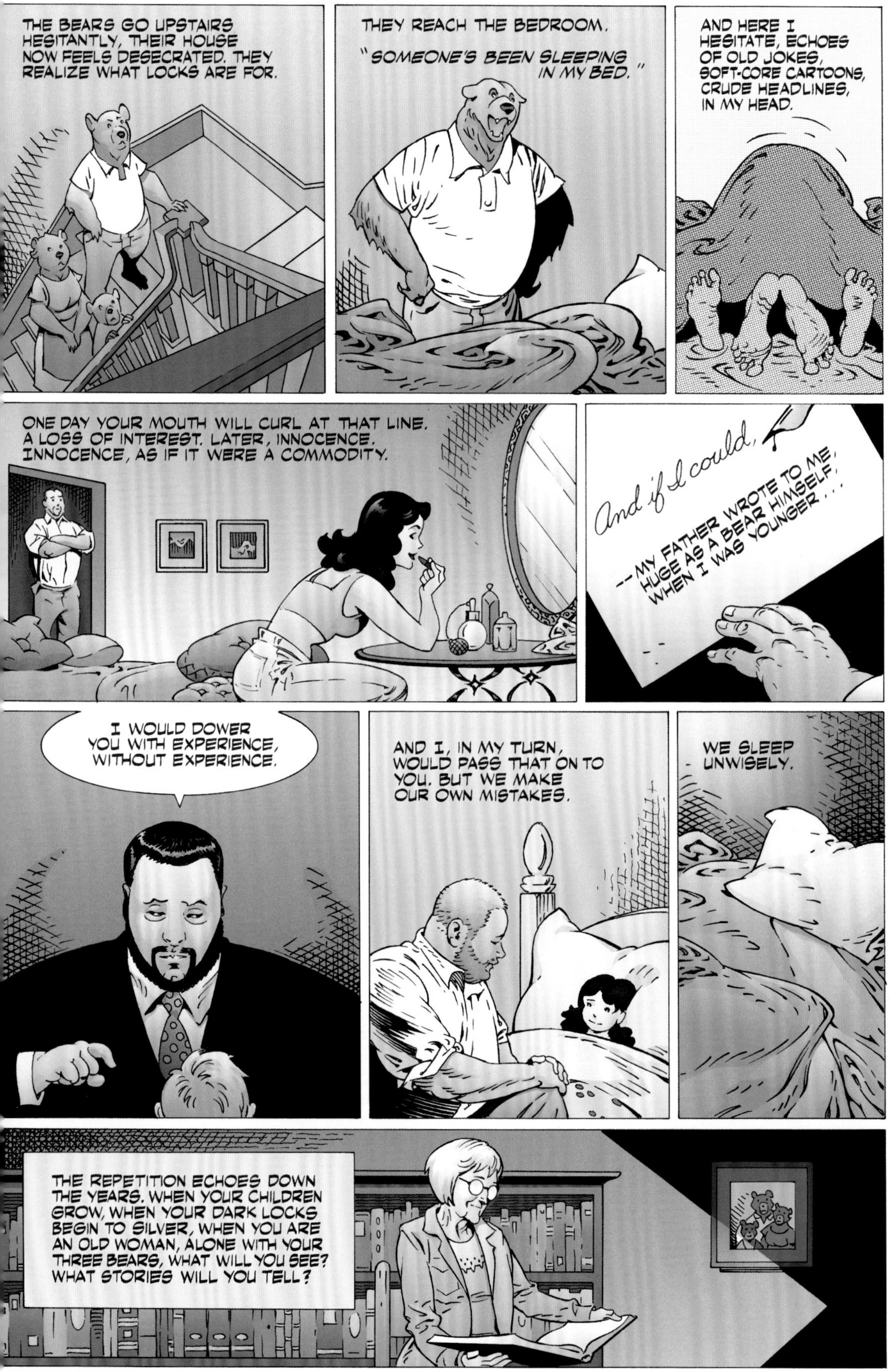
THE BEARS GO UPSTAIRS HESITANTLY, THEIR HOUSE NOW FEELS DESECRATED. THEY REALIZE WHAT LOCKS ARE FOR.
THEY REACH THE BEDROOM.
"SOMEONE'S BEEN SLEEPING IN MY BED."
AND HERE I HESITATE, ECHOES OF OLD JOKES, SOFT-CORE CARTOONS, CRUDE HEADLINES, IN MY HEAD.
ONE DAY YOUR MOUTH WILL CURL AT THAT LINE. A LOSS OF INTEREST. LATER, INNOCENCE. INNOCENCE, AS IF IT WERE A COMMODITY.
And if I could,
--MY FATHER WROTE TO ME, HUGE AS A BEAR HIMSELF, WHEN I WAS YOUNGER...
I WOULD DOWER YOU WITH EXPERIENCE, WITHOUT EXPERIENCE.
AND I, IN MY TURN, WOULD PASS THAT ON TO YOU. BUT WE MAKE OUR OWN MISTAKES.
WE SLEEP UNWISELY.
THE REPETITION ECHOES DOWN THE YEARS. WHEN YOUR CHILDREN GROW, WHEN YOUR DARK LOCKS BEGIN TO SILVER, WHEN YOU ARE AN OLD WOMAN, ALONE WITH YOUR THREE BEARS, WHAT WILL YOU SEE? WHAT STORIES WILL YOU TELL?

"AND THEN GOLDILOCKS JUMPED OUT OF THE WINDOW AND SHE RAN--"

TOGETHER, NOW:

ALL THE WAY HOME.

AND THEN YOU SAY...

AGAIN. AGAIN. AGAIN.

WE OWE IT TO EACH OTHER TO TELL STORIES.

THESE DAYS, MY SYMPATHY'S WITH FATHER BEAR.

BEFORE I LEAVE MY HOUSE I LOCK THE DOOR...

...AND CHECK EACH BED AND CHAIR ON MY RETURN.

AGAIN.

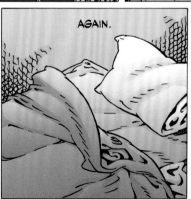

AGAIN.

AGAIN.

END

OCTOBER IN
THE CHAIR

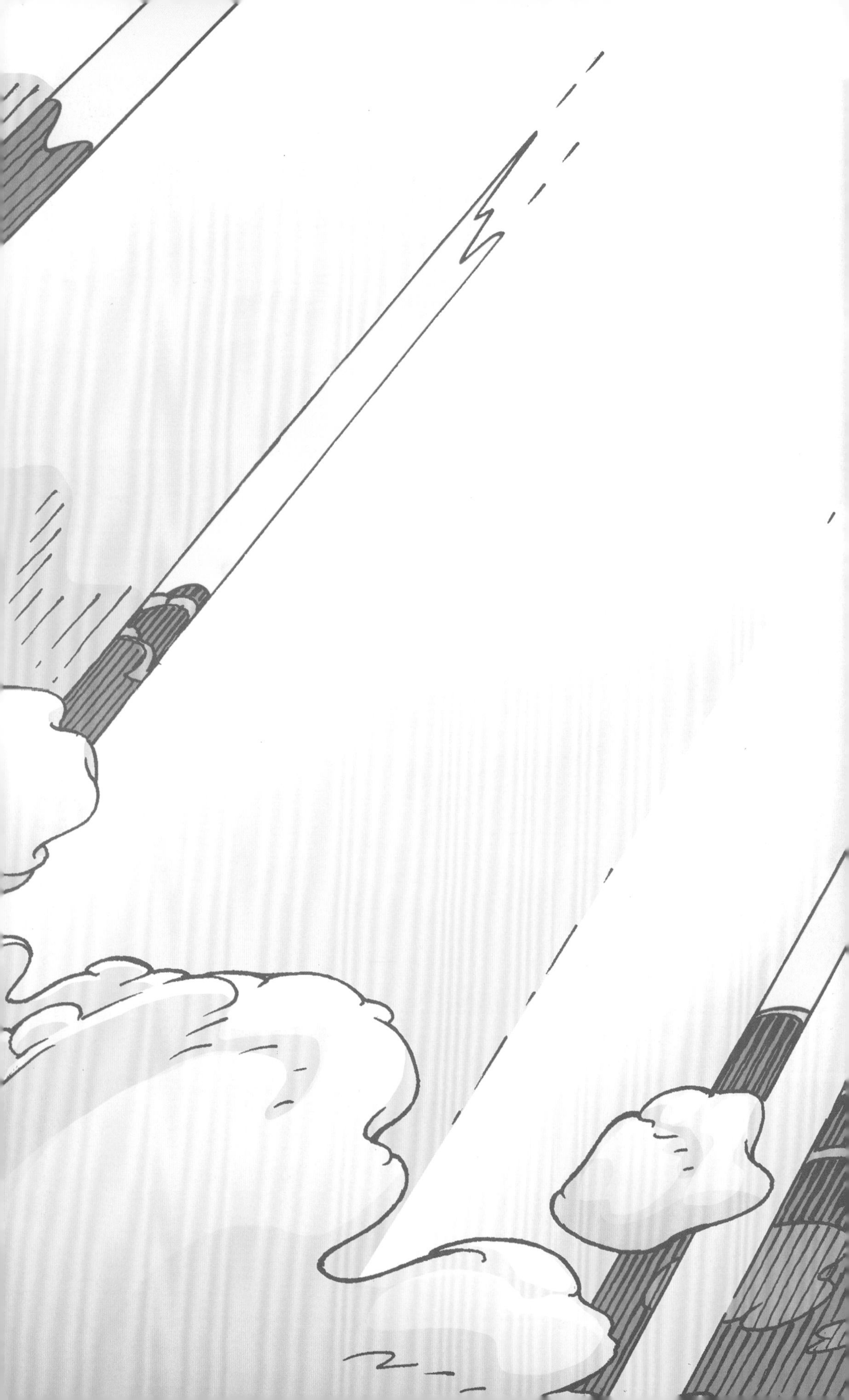

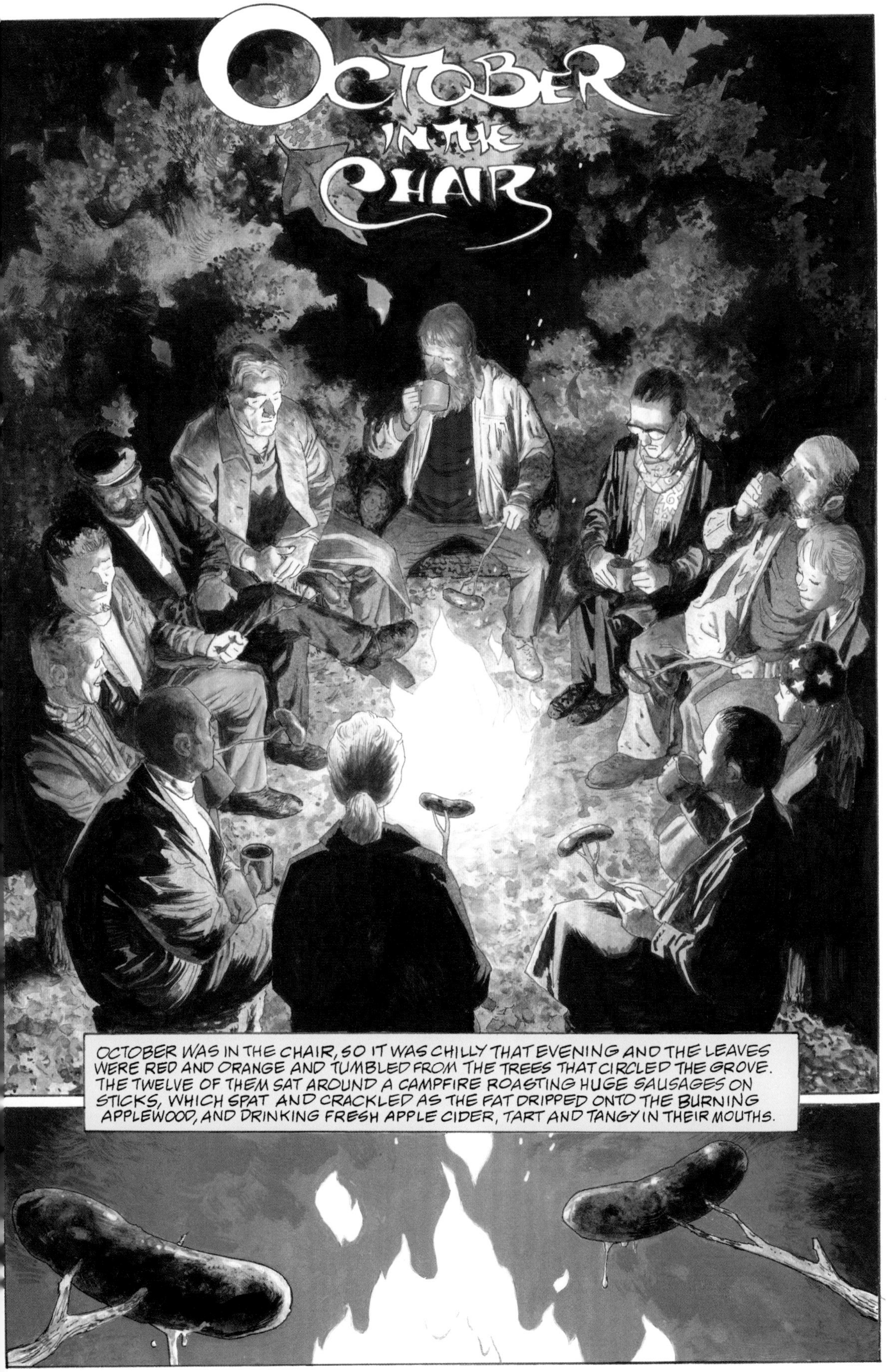
October in the Chair
OCTOBER WAS IN THE CHAIR, SO IT WAS CHILLY THAT EVENING AND THE LEAVES WERE RED AND ORANGE AND TUMBLED FROM THE TREES THAT CIRCLED THE GROVE. THE TWELVE OF THEM SAT AROUND A CAMPFIRE ROASTING HUGE SAUSAGES ON STICKS, WHICH SPAT AND CRACKLED AS THE FAT DRIPPED ONTO THE BURNING APPLEWOOD, AND DRINKING FRESH APPLE CIDER, TART AND TANGY IN THEIR MOUTHS.

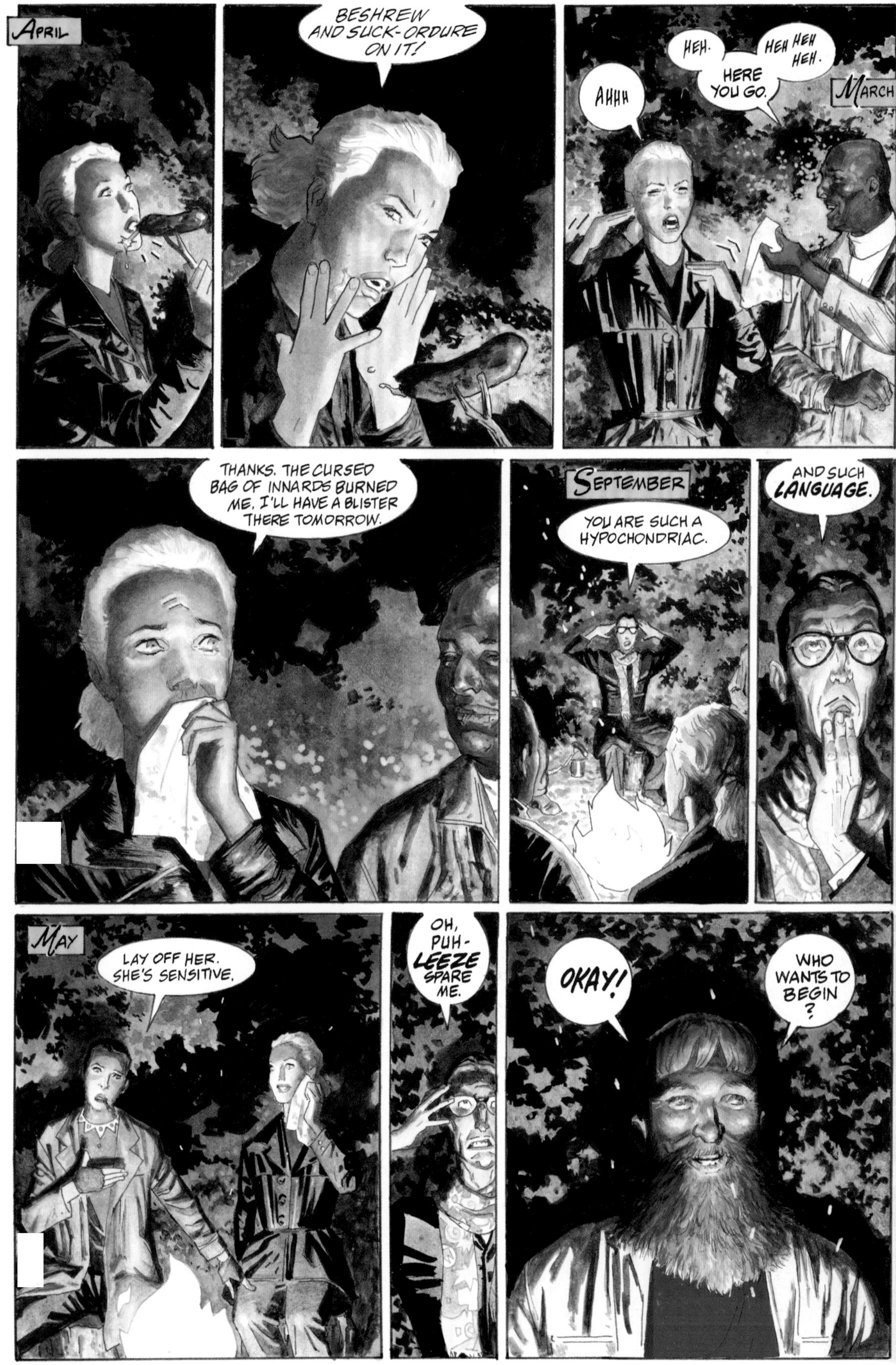
APRIL
BESHREW AND SUCK-ORDURE ON IT!
MARCH
AHHH
HEH.
HEH HEH HEH.
HERE YOU GO.
THANKS. THE CURSED BAG OF INNARDS BURNED ME. I'LL HAVE A BLISTER THERE TOMORROW.
SEPTEMBER
YOU ARE SUCH A HYPOCHONDRIAC.
AND SUCH LANGUAGE.
MAY
LAY OFF HER. SHE'S SENSITIVE.
OH, PUH-LEEZE SPARE ME.
OKAY!
WHO WANTS TO BEGIN?

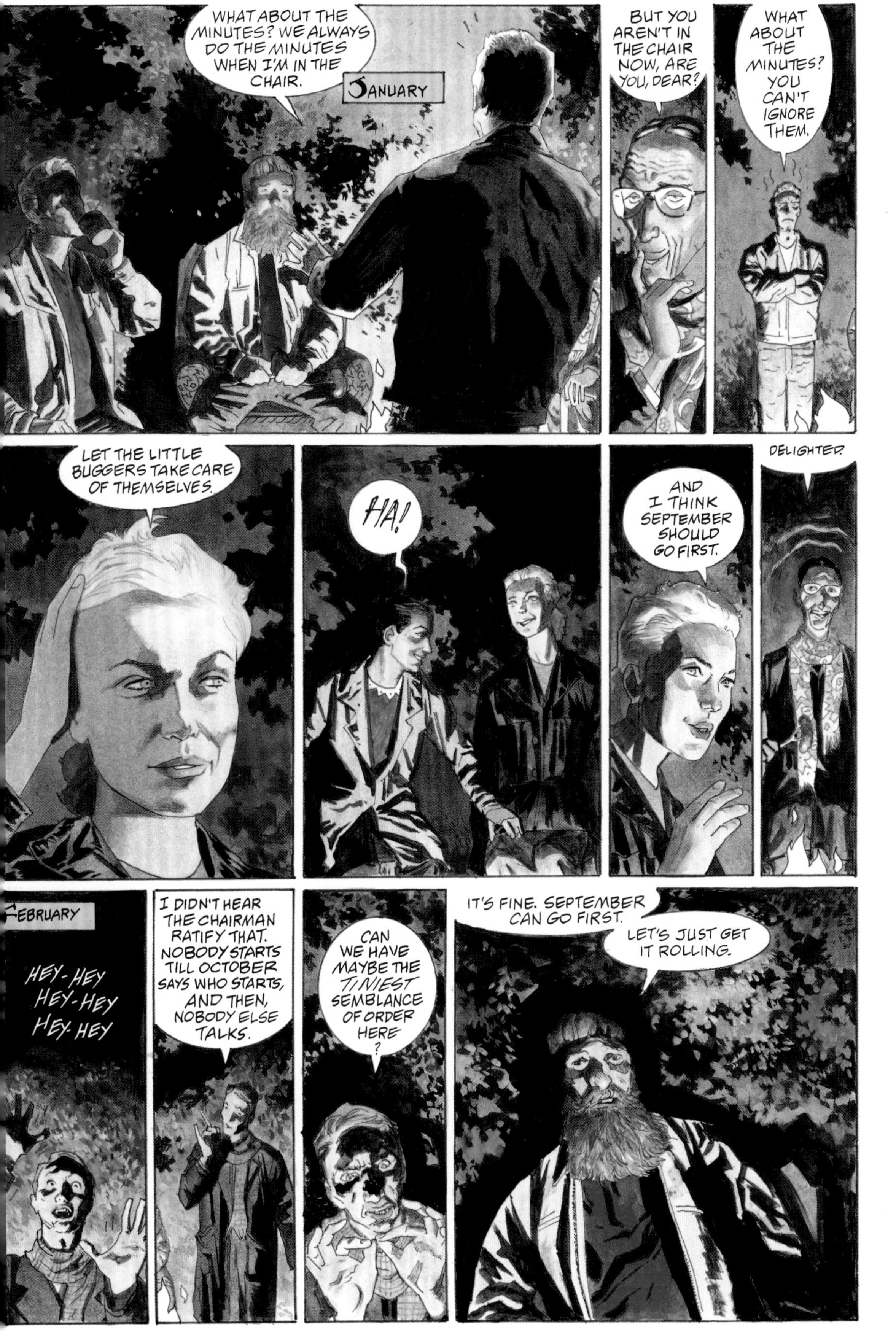
WHAT ABOUT THE MINUTES? WE ALWAYS DO THE MINUTES WHEN I'M IN THE CHAIR.
JANUARY
BUT YOU AREN'T IN THE CHAIR NOW, ARE YOU, DEAR?
WHAT ABOUT THE MINUTES? YOU CAN'T IGNORE THEM.
LET THE LITTLE BUGGERS TAKE CARE OF THEMSELVES.
HA!
AND I THINK SEPTEMBER SHOULD GO FIRST.
DELIGHTED.
FEBRUARY
HEY-HEY HEY-HEY HEY-HEY
I DIDN'T HEAR THE CHAIRMAN RATIFY THAT. NOBODY STARTS TILL OCTOBER SAYS WHO STARTS, AND THEN, NOBODY ELSE TALKS.
CAN WE HAVE MAYBE THE TINIEST SEMBLANCE OF ORDER HERE?
IT'S FINE. SEPTEMBER CAN GO FIRST.
LET'S JUST GET IT ROLLING.

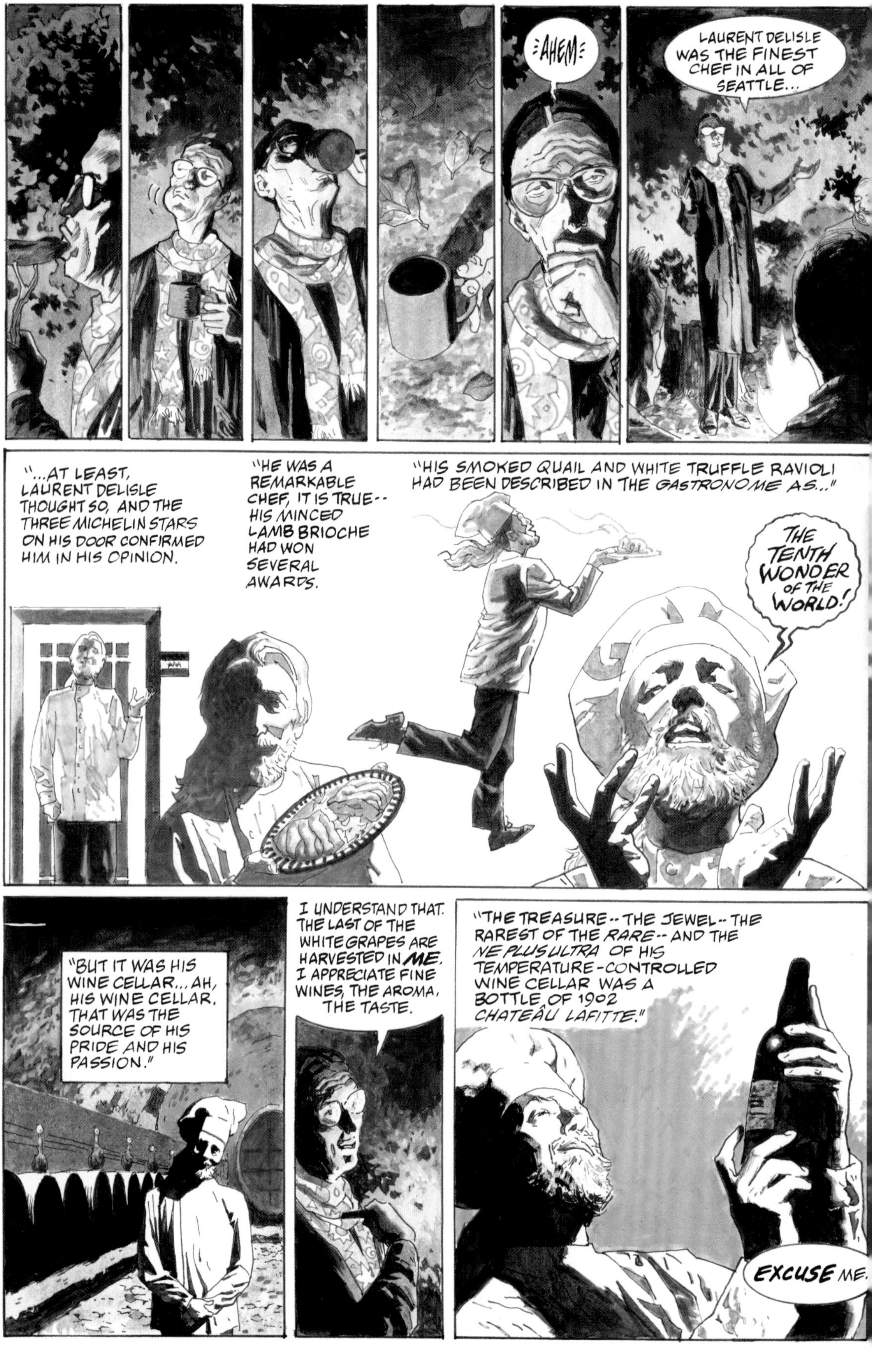

AHEM
LAURENT DELISLE WAS THE FINEST CHEF IN ALL OF SEATTLE...
"...AT LEAST, LAURENT DELISLE THOUGHT SO, AND THE THREE MICHELIN STARS ON HIS DOOR CONFIRMED HIM IN HIS OPINION.
"HE WAS A REMARKABLE CHEF, IT IS TRUE-- HIS MINCED LAMB BRIOCHE HAD WON SEVERAL AWARDS.
"HIS SMOKED QUAIL AND WHITE TRUFFLE RAVIOLI HAD BEEN DESCRIBED IN THE *GASTRONOME* AS..."
THE TENTH WONDER OF THE WORLD!
"BUT IT WAS HIS WINE CELLAR... AH, HIS WINE CELLAR. THAT WAS THE SOURCE OF HIS PRIDE AND HIS PASSION."
I UNDERSTAND THAT. THE LAST OF THE WHITE GRAPES ARE HARVESTED IN *ME*. I APPRECIATE FINE WINES, THE AROMA, THE TASTE.
"THE TREASURE -- THE JEWEL -- THE RAREST OF THE *RARE* -- AND THE *NE PLUS ULTRA* OF HIS TEMPERATURE-CONTROLLED WINE CELLAR WAS A BOTTLE OF 1902 *CHATEÂU LAFITTE*."
EXCUSE ME.

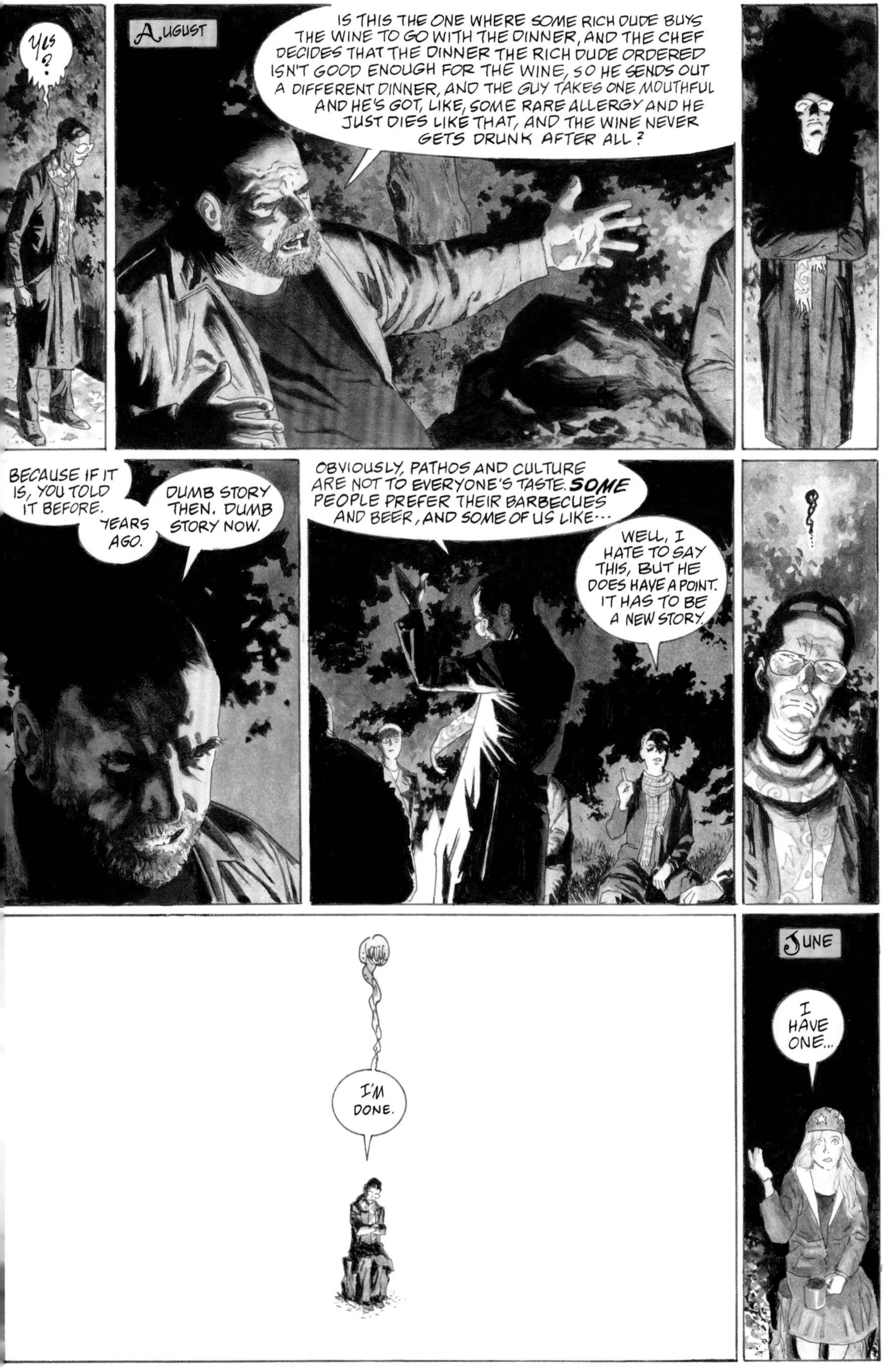
YES?
AUGUST
IS THIS THE ONE WHERE SOME RICH DUDE BUYS THE WINE TO GO WITH THE DINNER, AND THE CHEF DECIDES THAT THE DINNER THE RICH DUDE ORDERED ISN'T GOOD ENOUGH FOR THE WINE, SO HE SENDS OUT A DIFFERENT DINNER, AND THE GUY TAKES ONE MOUTHFUL AND HE'S GOT, LIKE, SOME RARE ALLERGY AND HE JUST DIES LIKE THAT, AND THE WINE NEVER GETS DRUNK AFTER ALL?
BECAUSE IF IT IS, YOU TOLD IT BEFORE.
YEARS AGO.
DUMB STORY THEN. DUMB STORY NOW.
OBVIOUSLY, PATHOS AND CULTURE ARE NOT TO EVERYONE'S TASTE. SOME PEOPLE PREFER THEIR BARBECUES AND BEER, AND SOME OF US LIKE...
WELL, I HATE TO SAY THIS, BUT HE DOES HAVE A POINT. IT HAS TO BE A NEW STORY.
?
I'M DONE.
JUNE
I HAVE ONE...

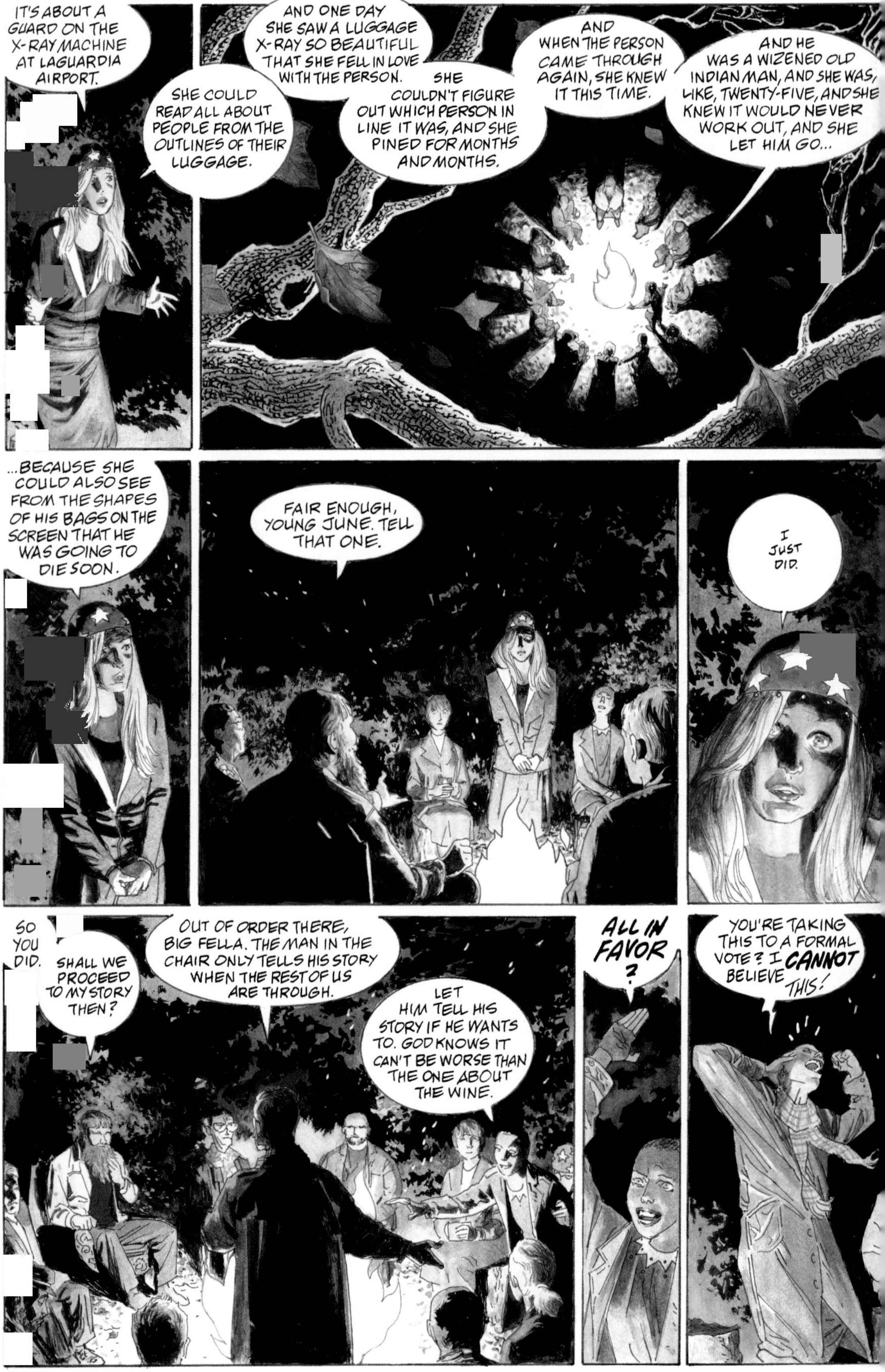
IT'S ABOUT A GUARD ON THE X-RAY MACHINE AT LAGUARDIA AIRPORT.
SHE COULD READ ALL ABOUT PEOPLE FROM THE OUTLINES OF THEIR LUGGAGE.
AND ONE DAY SHE SAW A LUGGAGE X-RAY SO BEAUTIFUL THAT SHE FELL IN LOVE WITH THE PERSON.
SHE COULDN'T FIGURE OUT WHICH PERSON IN LINE IT WAS, AND SHE PINED FOR MONTHS AND MONTHS.
AND WHEN THE PERSON CAME THROUGH AGAIN, SHE KNEW IT THIS TIME.
AND HE WAS A WIZENED OLD INDIAN MAN, AND SHE WAS, LIKE, TWENTY-FIVE, AND SHE KNEW IT WOULD NEVER WORK OUT, AND SHE LET HIM GO...
...BECAUSE SHE COULD ALSO SEE FROM THE SHAPES OF HIS BAGS ON THE SCREEN THAT HE WAS GOING TO DIE SOON.
FAIR ENOUGH, YOUNG JUNE. TELL THAT ONE.
I JUST DID.
SO YOU DID.
SHALL WE PROCEED TO MY STORY THEN?
OUT OF ORDER THERE, BIG FELLA. THE MAN IN THE CHAIR ONLY TELLS HIS STORY WHEN THE REST OF US ARE THROUGH.
LET HIM TELL HIS STORY IF HE WANTS TO. GOD KNOWS IT CAN'T BE WORSE THAN THE ONE ABOUT THE WINE.
ALL IN FAVOR?
YOU'RE TAKING THIS TO A FORMAL VOTE? I CANNOT BELIEVE THIS!

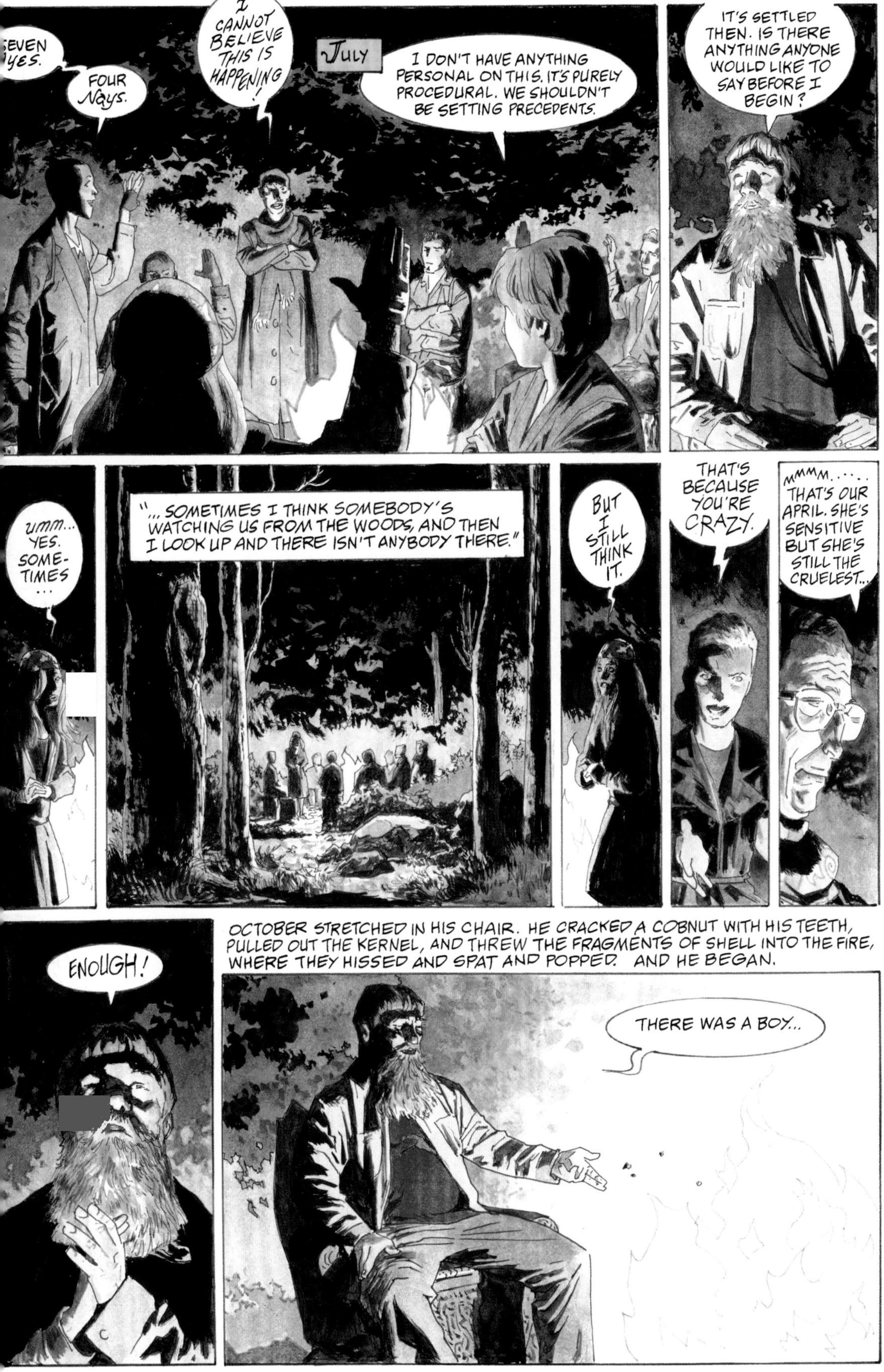
SEVEN YES.
FOUR NAYS.
I CANNOT BELIEVE THIS IS HAPPENING!
JULY
I DON'T HAVE ANYTHING PERSONAL ON THIS. IT'S PURELY PROCEDURAL. WE SHOULDN'T BE SETTING PRECEDENTS.
IT'S SETTLED THEN. IS THERE ANYTHING ANYONE WOULD LIKE TO SAY BEFORE I BEGIN?
UMM... YES. SOME-TIMES...
"...SOMETIMES I THINK SOMEBODY'S WATCHING US FROM THE WOODS, AND THEN I LOOK UP AND THERE ISN'T ANYBODY THERE."
BUT I STILL THINK IT.
THAT'S BECAUSE YOU'RE CRAZY.
MMMM..... THAT'S OUR APRIL. SHE'S SENSITIVE BUT SHE'S STILL THE CRUELEST...
ENOUGH!
OCTOBER STRETCHED IN HIS CHAIR. HE CRACKED A COBNUT WITH HIS TEETH, PULLED OUT THE KERNEL, AND THREW THE FRAGMENTS OF SHELL INTO THE FIRE, WHERE THEY HISSED AND SPAT AND POPPED. AND HE BEGAN.
THERE WAS A BOY...

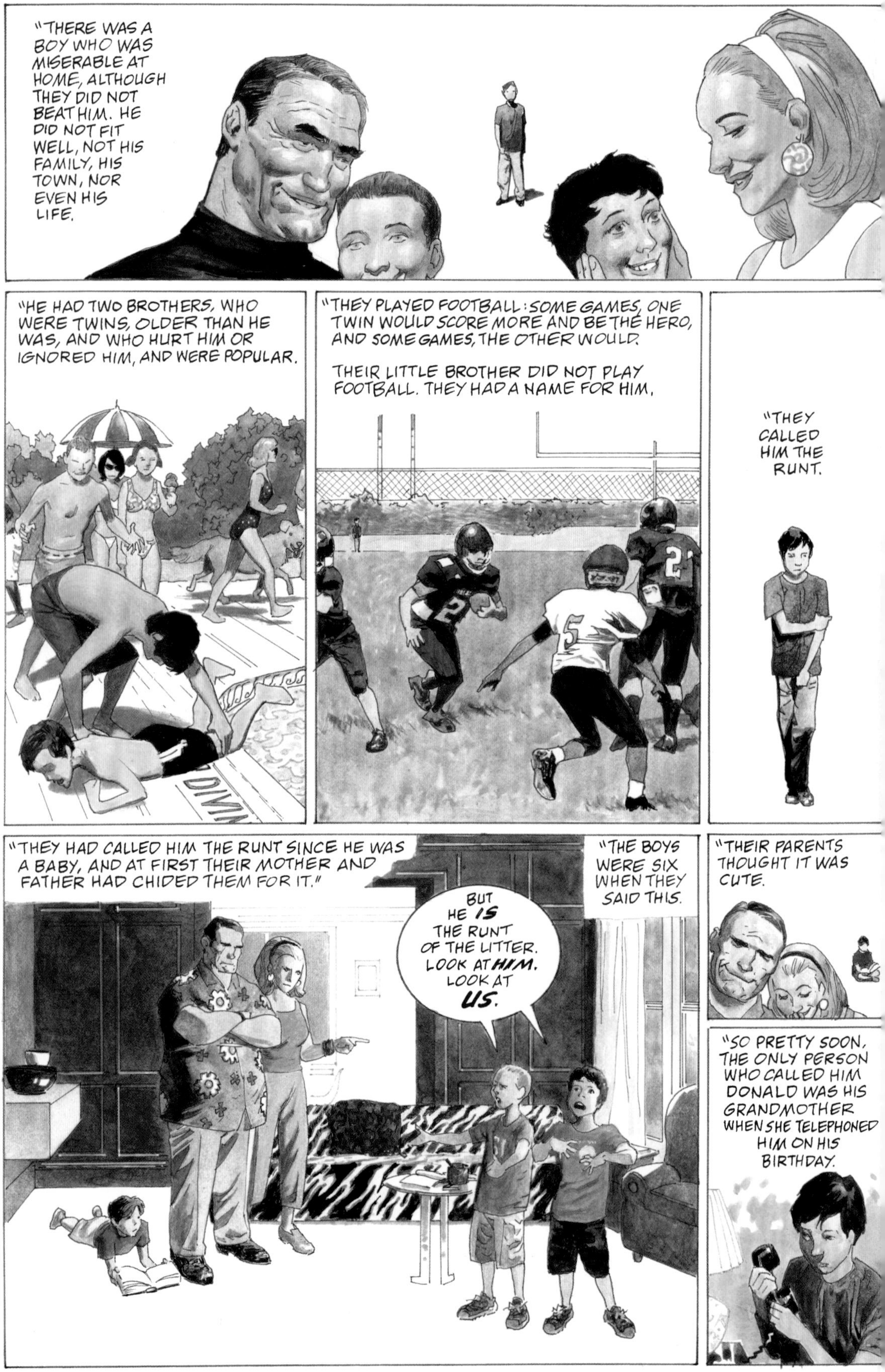
"THERE WAS A BOY WHO WAS MISERABLE AT HOME, ALTHOUGH THEY DID NOT BEAT HIM. HE DID NOT FIT WELL, NOT HIS FAMILY, HIS TOWN, NOR EVEN HIS LIFE.
"HE HAD TWO BROTHERS, WHO WERE TWINS, OLDER THAN HE WAS, AND WHO HURT HIM OR IGNORED HIM, AND WERE POPULAR.
"THEY PLAYED FOOTBALL: SOME GAMES, ONE TWIN WOULD SCORE MORE AND BE THE HERO, AND SOME GAMES, THE OTHER WOULD.
THEIR LITTLE BROTHER DID NOT PLAY FOOTBALL. THEY HAD A NAME FOR HIM.
"THEY CALLED HIM THE RUNT.
"THEY HAD CALLED HIM THE RUNT SINCE HE WAS A BABY, AND AT FIRST THEIR MOTHER AND FATHER HAD CHIDED THEM FOR IT."
"THE BOYS WERE SIX WHEN THEY SAID THIS.
BUT HE IS THE RUNT OF THE LITTER. LOOK AT HIM. LOOK AT US.
"THEIR PARENTS THOUGHT IT WAS CUTE.
"SO PRETTY SOON, THE ONLY PERSON WHO CALLED HIM DONALD WAS HIS GRANDMOTHER WHEN SHE TELEPHONED HIM ON HIS BIRTHDAY.

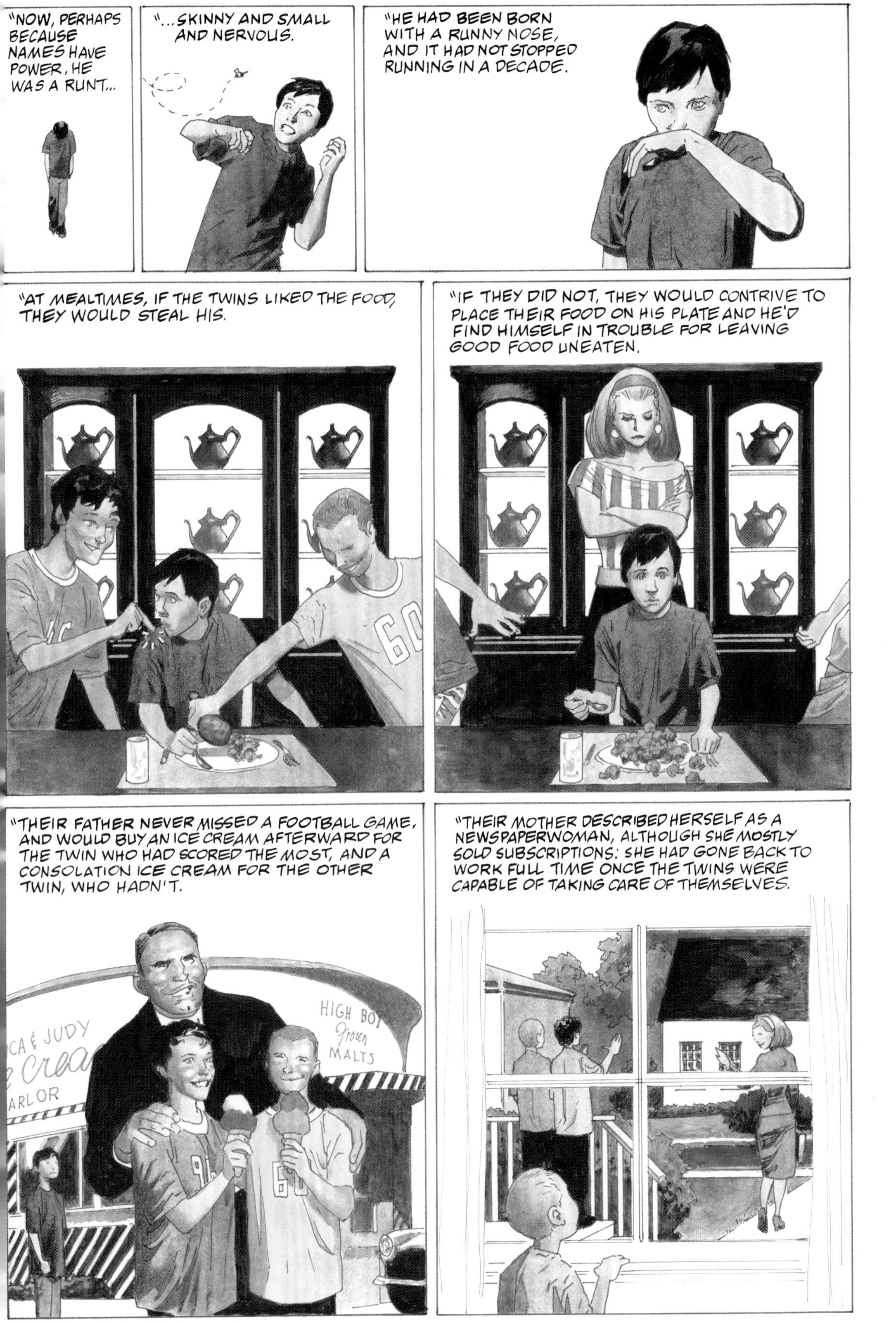
"NOW, PERHAPS BECAUSE NAMES HAVE POWER, HE WAS A RUNT...
"...SKINNY AND SMALL AND NERVOUS.
"HE HAD BEEN BORN WITH A RUNNY NOSE, AND IT HAD NOT STOPPED RUNNING IN A DECADE.
"AT MEALTIMES, IF THE TWINS LIKED THE FOOD, THEY WOULD STEAL HIS.
"IF THEY DID NOT, THEY WOULD CONTRIVE TO PLACE THEIR FOOD ON HIS PLATE AND HE'D FIND HIMSELF IN TROUBLE FOR LEAVING GOOD FOOD UNEATEN.
"THEIR FATHER NEVER MISSED A FOOTBALL GAME, AND WOULD BUY AN ICE CREAM AFTERWARD FOR THE TWIN WHO HAD SCORED THE MOST, AND A CONSOLATION ICE CREAM FOR THE OTHER TWIN, WHO HADN'T.
CA & JUDY
ARLOR
HIGH BOY
Frozen
MALTS
"THEIR MOTHER DESCRIBED HERSELF AS A NEWSPAPERWOMAN, ALTHOUGH SHE MOSTLY SOLD SUBSCRIPTIONS: SHE HAD GONE BACK TO WORK FULL TIME ONCE THE TWINS WERE CAPABLE OF TAKING CARE OF THEMSELVES.

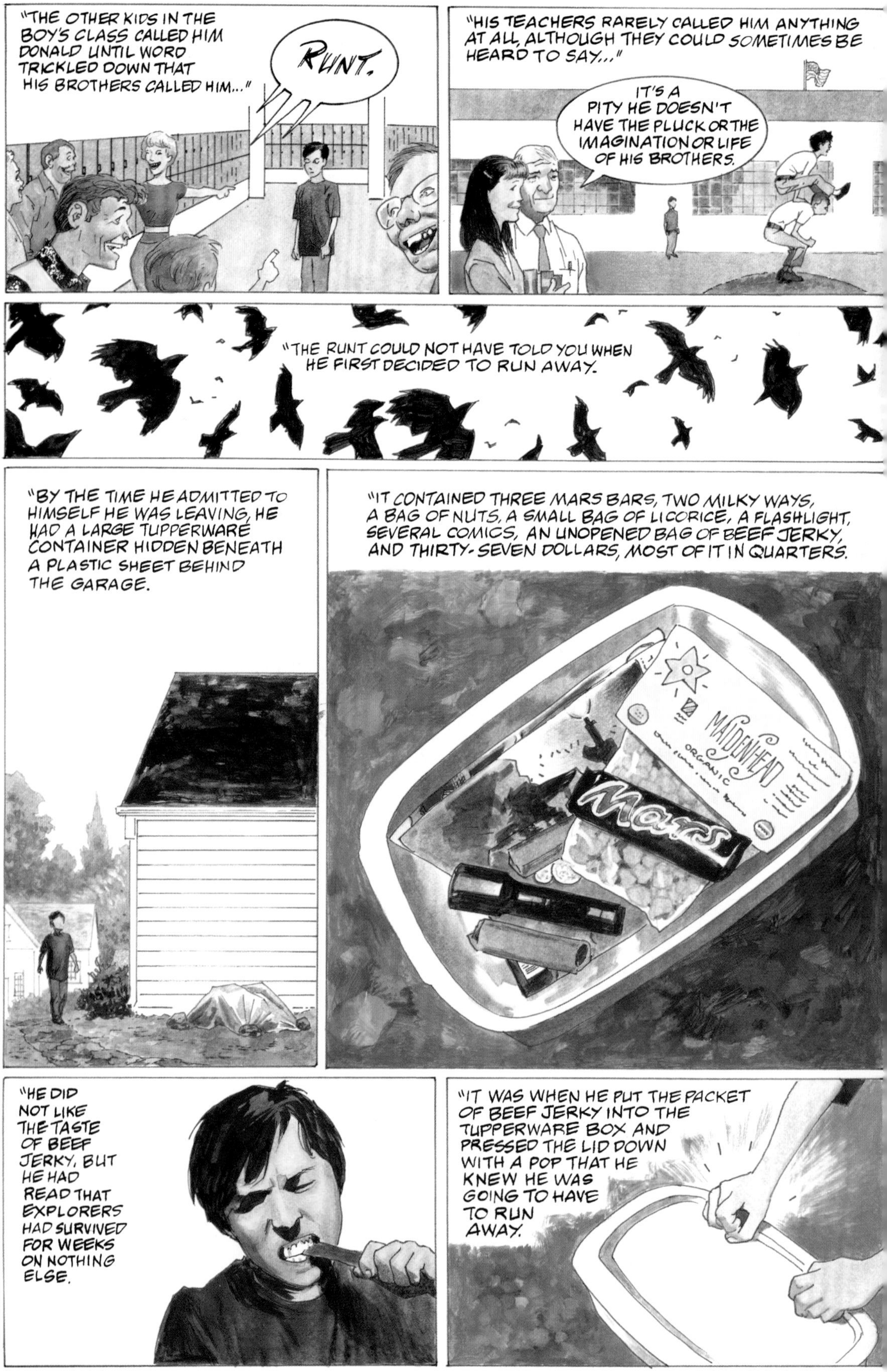
"THE OTHER KIDS IN THE BOY'S CLASS CALLED HIM DONALD UNTIL WORD TRICKLED DOWN THAT HIS BROTHERS CALLED HIM..."
RUNT.
"HIS TEACHERS RARELY CALLED HIM ANYTHING AT ALL, ALTHOUGH THEY COULD SOMETIMES BE HEARD TO SAY..."
IT'S A PITY HE DOESN'T HAVE THE PLUCK OR THE IMAGINATION OR LIFE OF HIS BROTHERS.
"THE RUNT COULD NOT HAVE TOLD YOU WHEN HE FIRST DECIDED TO RUN AWAY.
"BY THE TIME HE ADMITTED TO HIMSELF HE WAS LEAVING, HE HAD A LARGE TUPPERWARE CONTAINER HIDDEN BENEATH A PLASTIC SHEET BEHIND THE GARAGE.
"IT CONTAINED THREE MARS BARS, TWO MILKY WAYS, A BAG OF NUTS, A SMALL BAG OF LICORICE, A FLASHLIGHT, SEVERAL COMICS, AN UNOPENED BAG OF BEEF JERKY, AND THIRTY-SEVEN DOLLARS, MOST OF IT IN QUARTERS.
MAIDENHEAD
ORGANIC
Mars
"HE DID NOT LIKE THE TASTE OF BEEF JERKY, BUT HE HAD READ THAT EXPLORERS HAD SURVIVED FOR WEEKS ON NOTHING ELSE.
"IT WAS WHEN HE PUT THE PACKET OF BEEF JERKY INTO THE TUPPERWARE BOX AND PRESSED THE LID DOWN WITH A POP THAT HE KNEW HE WAS GOING TO HAVE TO RUN AWAY.

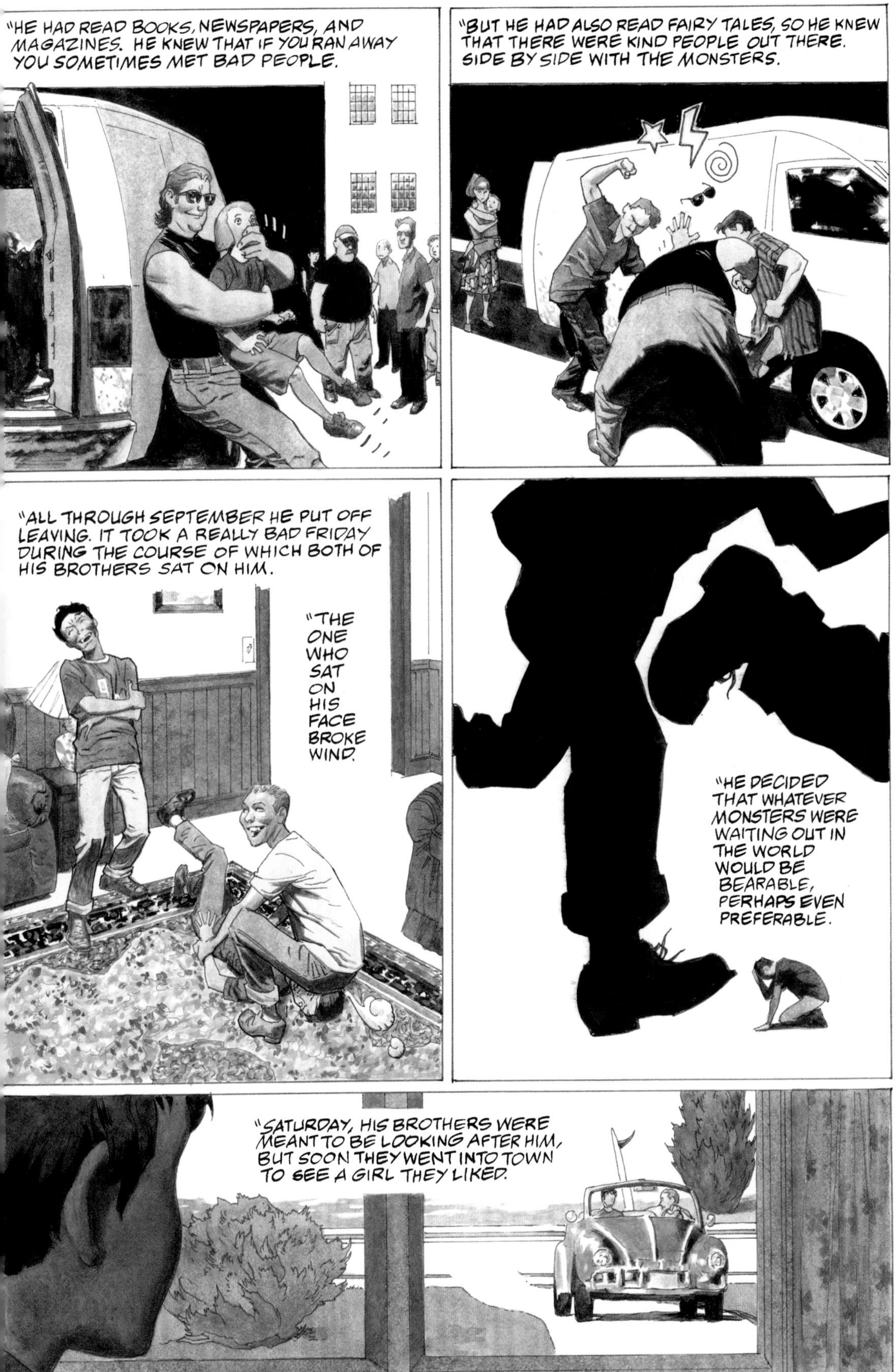
"HE HAD READ BOOKS, NEWSPAPERS, AND MAGAZINES. HE KNEW THAT IF YOU RAN AWAY YOU SOMETIMES MET BAD PEOPLE.
"BUT HE HAD ALSO READ FAIRY TALES, SO HE KNEW THAT THERE WERE KIND PEOPLE OUT THERE. SIDE BY SIDE WITH THE MONSTERS.
"ALL THROUGH SEPTEMBER HE PUT OFF LEAVING. IT TOOK A REALLY BAD FRIDAY DURING THE COURSE OF WHICH BOTH OF HIS BROTHERS SAT ON HIM.
"THE ONE WHO SAT ON HIS FACE BROKE WIND.
"HE DECIDED THAT WHATEVER MONSTERS WERE WAITING OUT IN THE WORLD WOULD BE BEARABLE, PERHAPS EVEN PREFERABLE.
"SATURDAY, HIS BROTHERS WERE MEANT TO BE LOOKING AFTER HIM, BUT SOON THEY WENT INTO TOWN TO SEE A GIRL THEY LIKED.

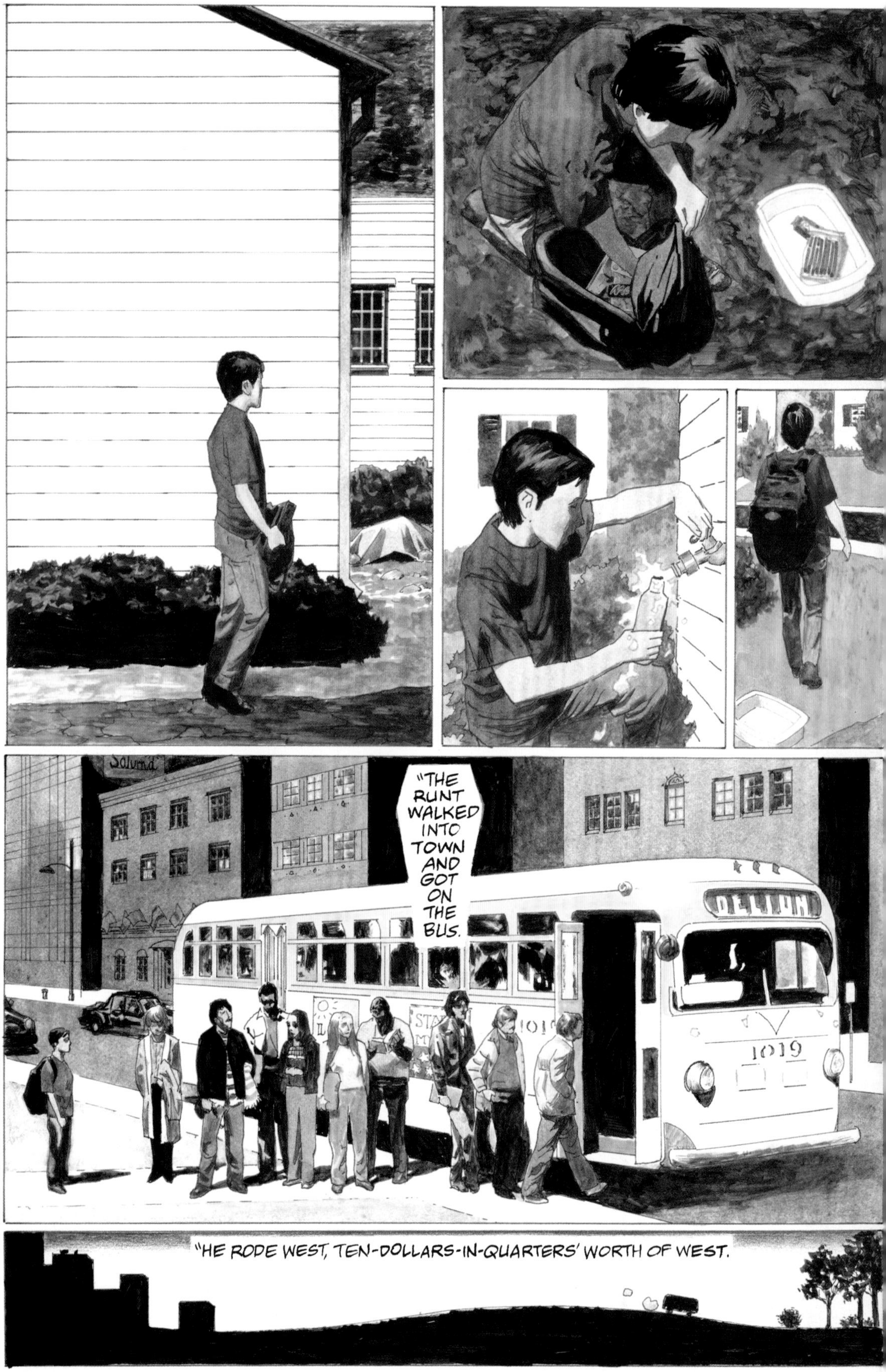
"THE RUNT WALKED INTO TOWN AND GOT ON THE BUS.
"HE RODE WEST, TEN-DOLLARS-IN-QUARTERS' WORTH OF WEST.

"THEN HE GOT OFF THE BUS.

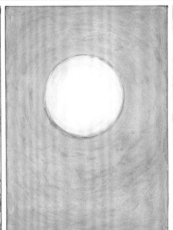

"HE HAD THOUGHT THAT ONCE HE GOT OUT OF TOWN HE WOULD SEE SPRINGS OF FRESH WATER EVERYWHERE BUT THERE WERE NONE TO BE FOUND. HE REMEMBERED SOMETHING HE HAD BEEN TOLD IN SCHOOL..."

IN THE END, ALL RIVERS FLOW INTO THE SEA.

I'VE NEVER BEEN TO THE SEASHORE.

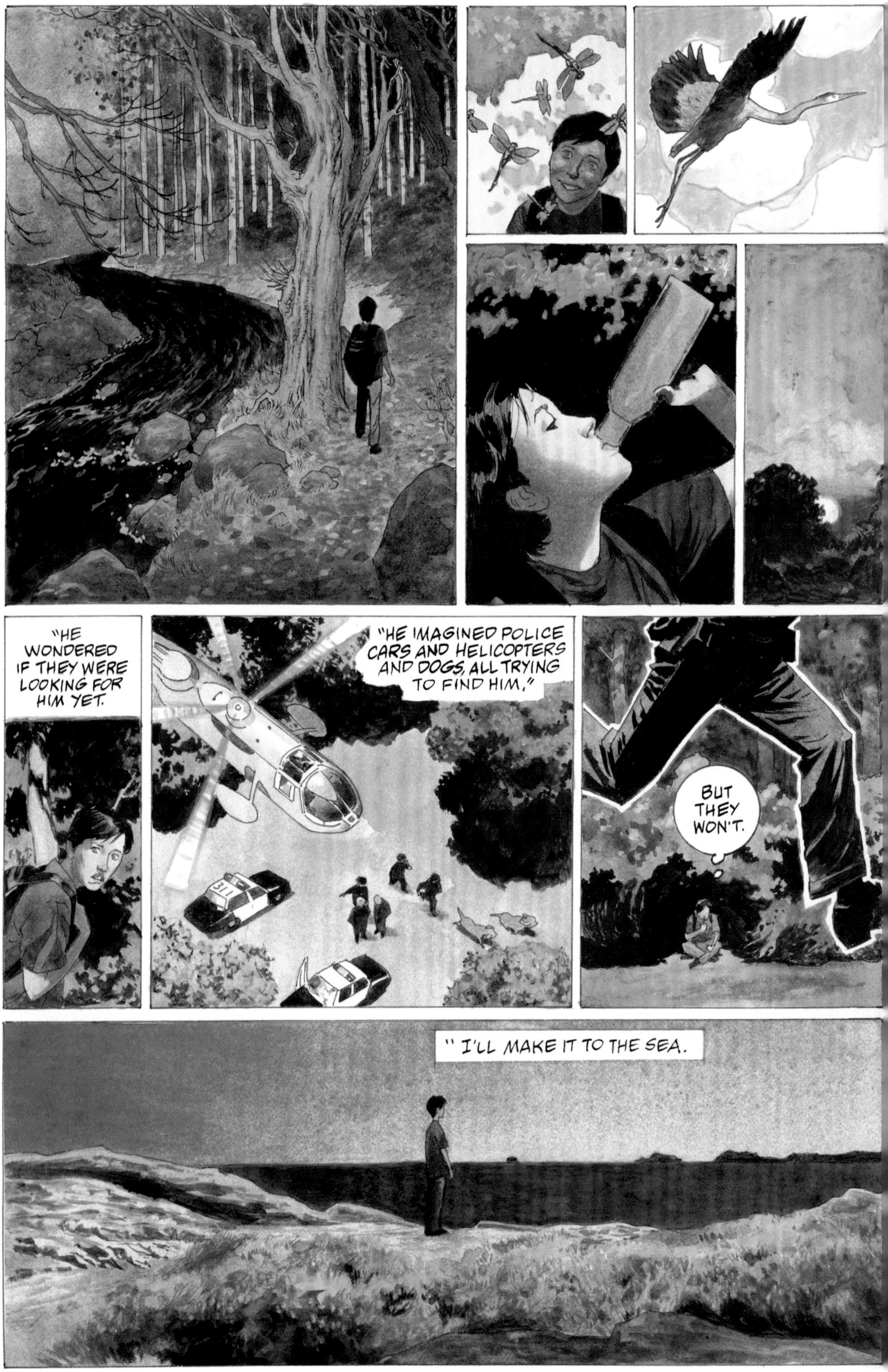
"HE WONDERED IF THEY WERE LOOKING FOR HIM YET.
"HE IMAGINED POLICE CARS AND HELICOPTERS AND DOGS, ALL TRYING TO FIND HIM."
BUT THEY WON'T.
" I'LL MAKE IT TO THE SEA.

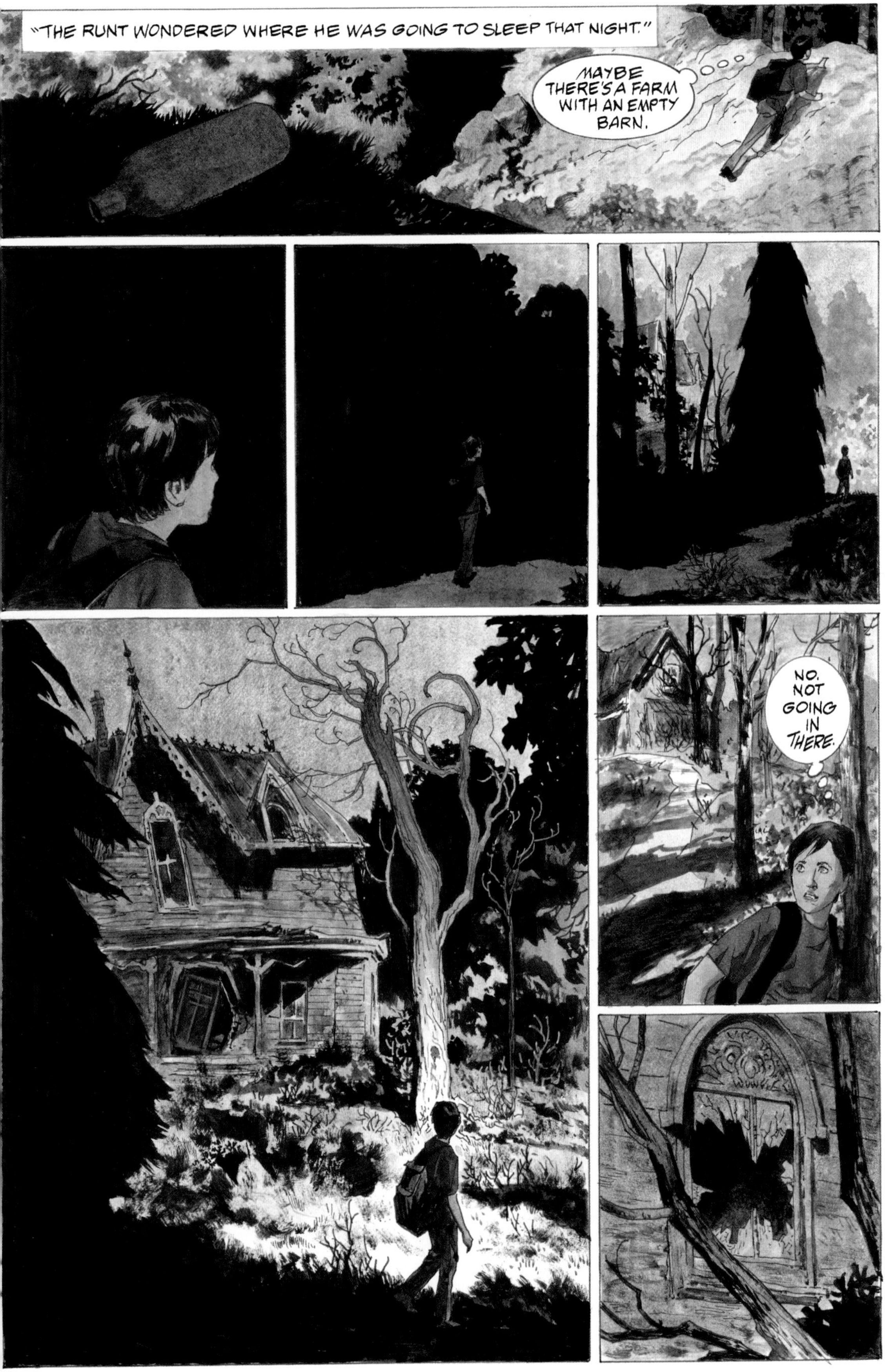
"THE RUNT WONDERED WHERE HE WAS GOING TO SLEEP THAT NIGHT."
MAYBE THERE'S A FARM WITH AN EMPTY BARN.
NO. NOT GOING IN THERE.

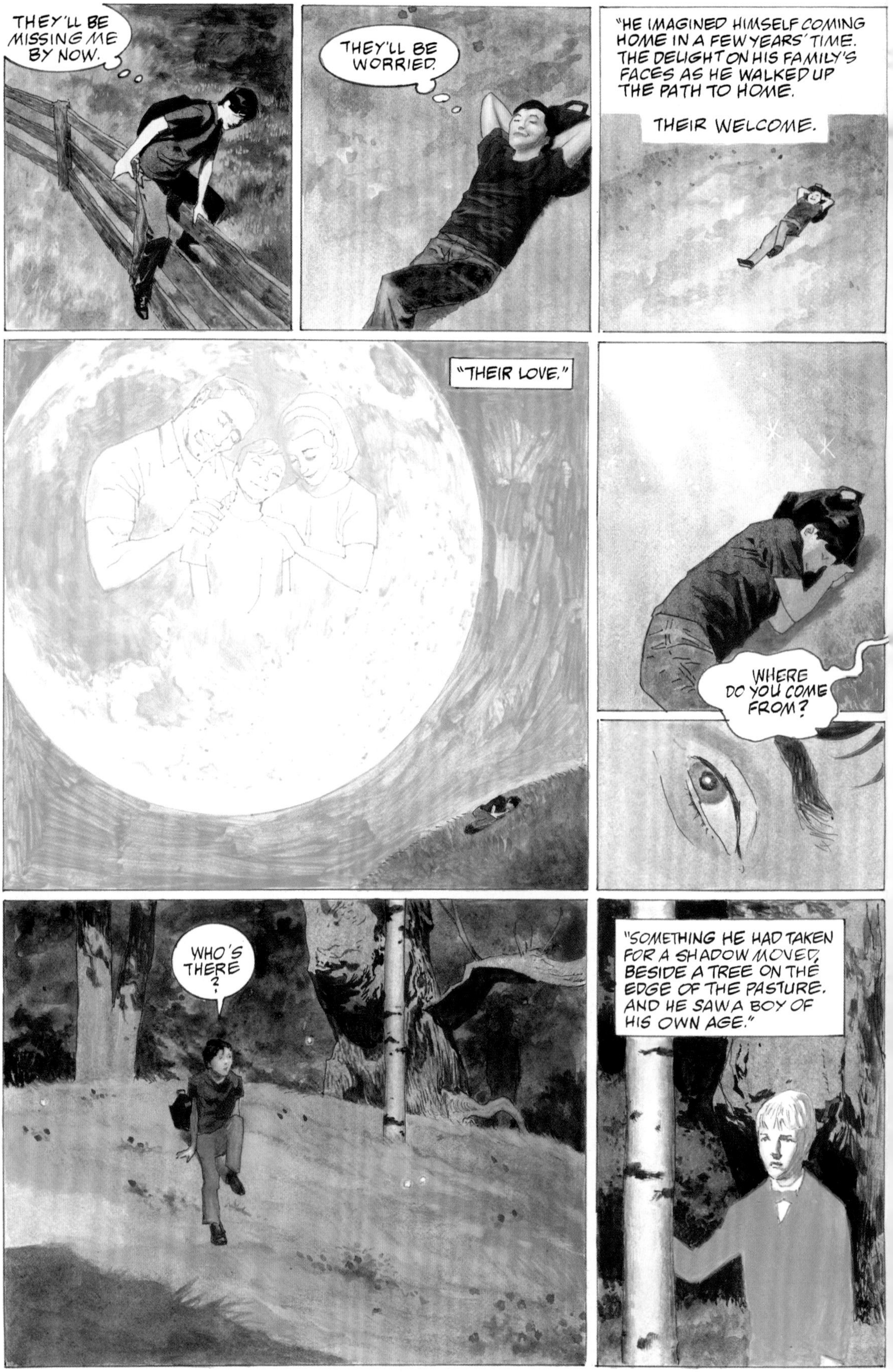
THEY'LL BE MISSING ME BY NOW.
THEY'LL BE WORRIED.
"HE IMAGINED HIMSELF COMING HOME IN A FEW YEARS' TIME. THE DELIGHT ON HIS FAMILY'S FACES AS HE WALKED UP THE PATH TO HOME.
THEIR WELCOME.
"THEIR LOVE."
WHERE DO YOU COME FROM?
WHO'S THERE?
"SOMETHING HE HAD TAKEN FOR A SHADOW MOVED, BESIDE A TREE ON THE EDGE OF THE PASTURE. AND HE SAW A BOY OF HIS OWN AGE."

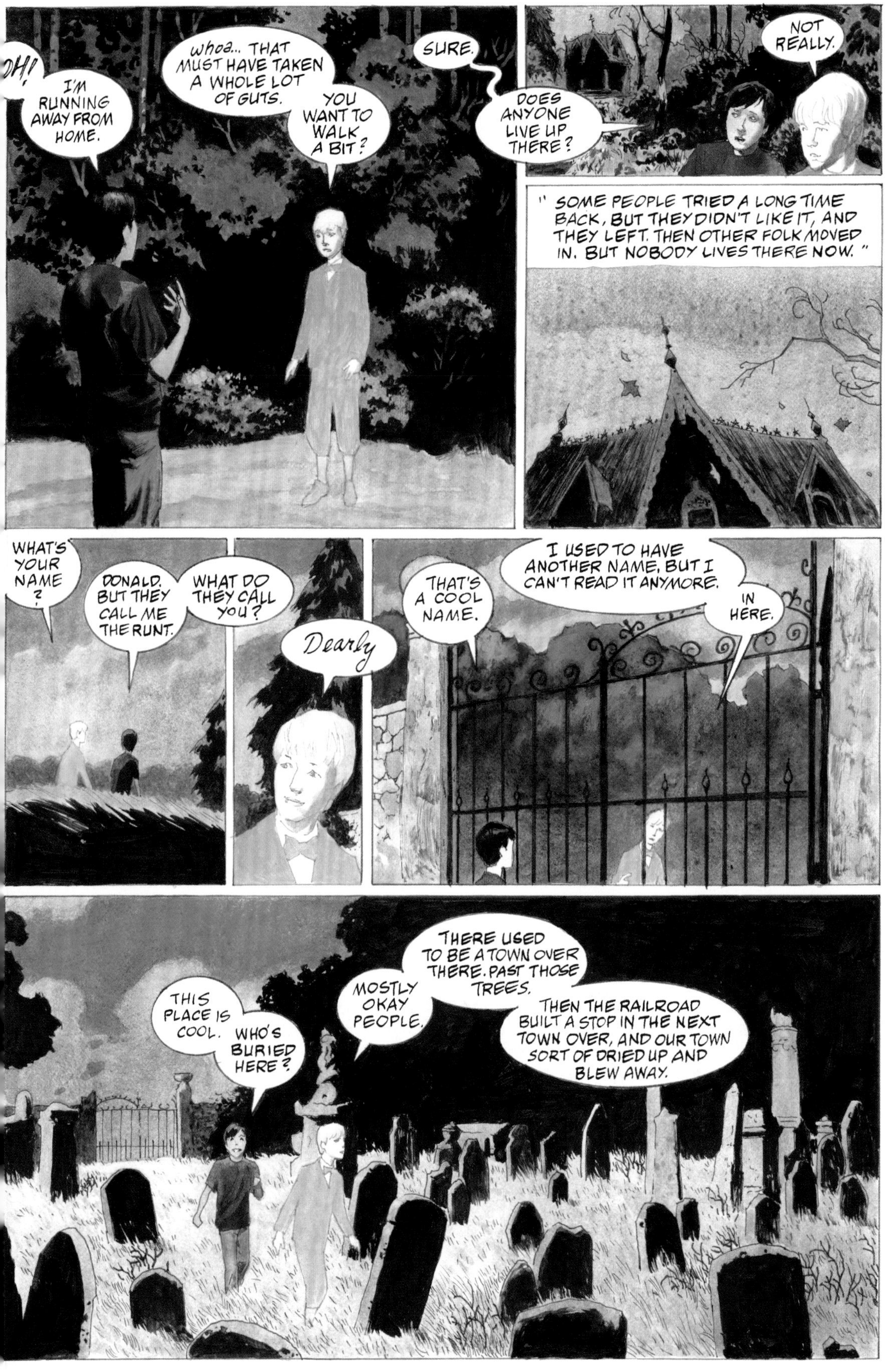
OH!
I'M RUNNING AWAY FROM HOME.
Whoa... THAT MUST HAVE TAKEN A WHOLE LOT OF GUTS.
YOU WANT TO WALK A BIT?
SURE.
DOES ANYONE LIVE UP THERE?
NOT REALLY.
" SOME PEOPLE TRIED A LONG TIME BACK, BUT THEY DIDN'T LIKE IT, AND THEY LEFT. THEN OTHER FOLK MOVED IN. BUT NOBODY LIVES THERE NOW. "
WHAT'S YOUR NAME?
DONALD. BUT THEY CALL ME THE RUNT.
WHAT DO THEY CALL YOU?
Dearly
THAT'S A COOL NAME.
I USED TO HAVE ANOTHER NAME, BUT I CAN'T READ IT ANYMORE.
IN HERE.
THIS PLACE IS COOL.
WHO'S BURIED HERE?
MOSTLY OKAY PEOPLE.
THERE USED TO BE A TOWN OVER THERE. PAST THOSE TREES.
THEN THE RAILROAD BUILT A STOP IN THE NEXT TOWN OVER, AND OUR TOWN SORT OF DRIED UP AND BLEW AWAY.

YOU CAN HIDE IN THE TREES AND GO INTO THE HOUSES AND JUMP OUT.

ARE THEY LIKE THAT FARMHOUSE UP THERE? THE HOUSES? I DON'T WANT TO GO IN THEM IF THEY ARE.

NO, NOBODY GOES IN THEM, EXCEPT FOR ME. AND SOME ANIMALS SOMETIMES. I'M THE ONLY KID AROUND HERE.

MAYBE WE CAN GO DOWN AND PLAY IN THEM.

COOL.

"IT WAS A PERFECT OCTOBER NIGHT: ALMOST AS WARM AS SUMMER AND THE HARVEST MOON DOMINATED THE SKY. YOU COULD SEE EVERYTHING."

WHICH ONE IS YOURS?

HERE.

DEARLY DEPARTED · WILL NEVER BE FORGOTTEN

FORGOTTEN I'D WAGER!

YEAH, THAT'S WHAT I'D SAY, TOO.

LET'S GO.

"THEY WENT DOWN A GULLY AND INTO WHAT REMAINED OF THE OLD TOWN.

58

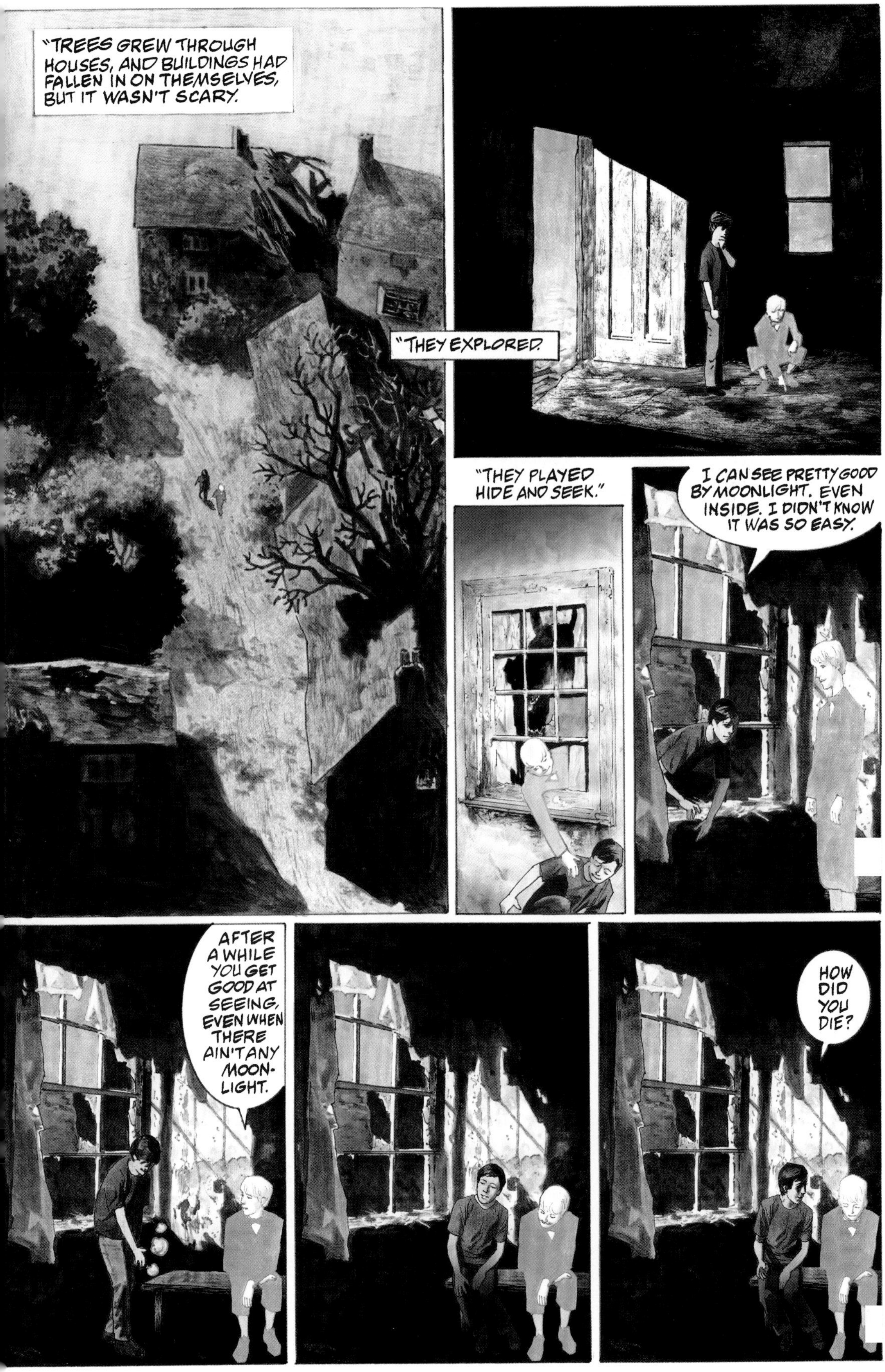
"TREES GREW THROUGH HOUSES, AND BUILDINGS HAD FALLEN IN ON THEMSELVES, BUT IT WASN'T SCARY.
"THEY EXPLORED.
"THEY PLAYED HIDE AND SEEK."
I CAN SEE PRETTY GOOD BY MOONLIGHT. EVEN INSIDE. I DIDN'T KNOW IT WAS SO EASY.
AFTER A WHILE YOU GET GOOD AT SEEING, EVEN WHEN THERE AIN'T ANY MOON-LIGHT.
HOW DID YOU DIE?

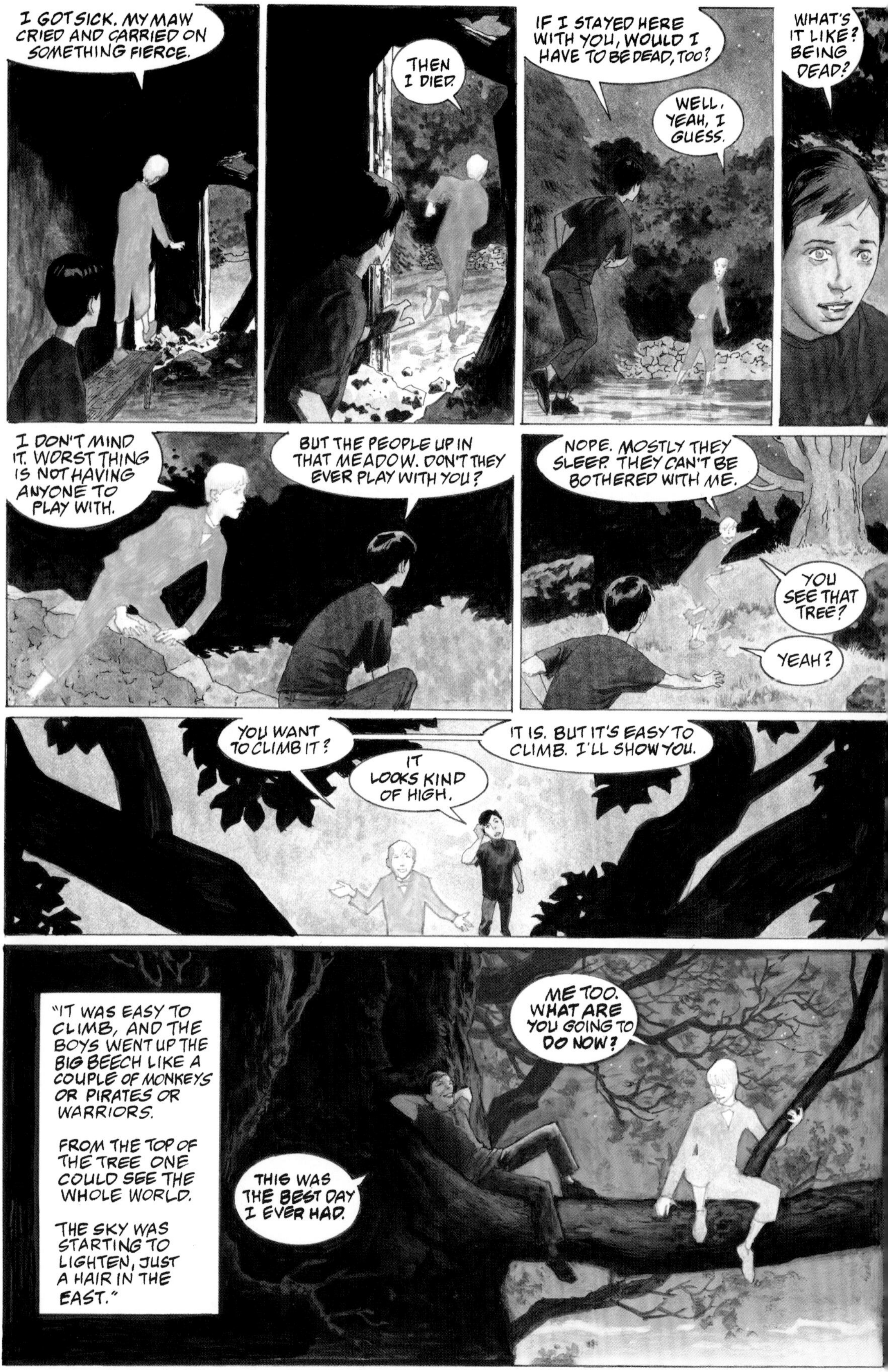
I GOT SICK. MY MAW CRIED AND CARRIED ON SOMETHING FIERCE.
THEN I DIED.
IF I STAYED HERE WITH YOU, WOULD I HAVE TO BE DEAD, TOO?
WELL, YEAH, I GUESS.
WHAT'S IT LIKE? BEING DEAD?
I DON'T MIND IT. WORST THING IS NOT HAVING ANYONE TO PLAY WITH.
BUT THE PEOPLE UP IN THAT MEADOW. DON'T THEY EVER PLAY WITH YOU?
NOPE. MOSTLY THEY SLEEP. THEY CAN'T BE BOTHERED WITH ME.
YOU SEE THAT TREE?
YEAH?
YOU WANT TO CLIMB IT?
IT LOOKS KIND OF HIGH.
IT IS. BUT IT'S EASY TO CLIMB. I'LL SHOW YOU.
"IT WAS EASY TO CLIMB, AND THE BOYS WENT UP THE BIG BEECH LIKE A COUPLE OF MONKEYS OR PIRATES OR WARRIORS.
FROM THE TOP OF THE TREE ONE COULD SEE THE WHOLE WORLD.
THE SKY WAS STARTING TO LIGHTEN, JUST A HAIR IN THE EAST."
THIS WAS THE BEST DAY I EVER HAD.
ME TOO. WHAT ARE YOU GOING TO DO NOW?

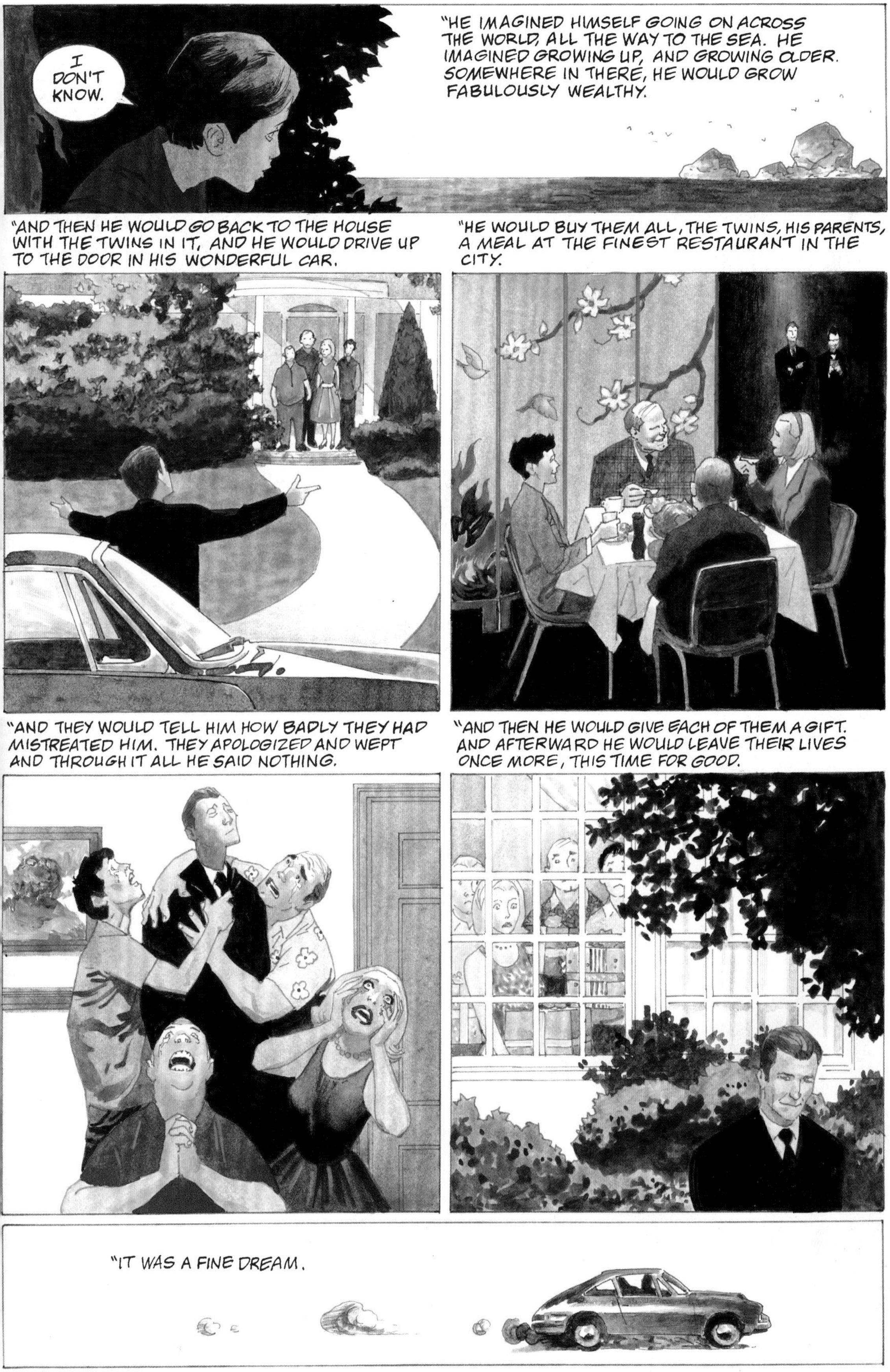
I DON'T KNOW.
"HE IMAGINED HIMSELF GOING ON ACROSS THE WORLD, ALL THE WAY TO THE SEA. HE IMAGINED GROWING UP, AND GROWING OLDER. SOMEWHERE IN THERE, HE WOULD GROW FABULOUSLY WEALTHY.
"AND THEN HE WOULD GO BACK TO THE HOUSE WITH THE TWINS IN IT, AND HE WOULD DRIVE UP TO THE DOOR IN HIS WONDERFUL CAR.
"HE WOULD BUY THEM ALL, THE TWINS, HIS PARENTS, A MEAL AT THE FINEST RESTAURANT IN THE CITY.
"AND THEY WOULD TELL HIM HOW BADLY THEY HAD MISTREATED HIM. THEY APOLOGIZED AND WEPT AND THROUGH IT ALL HE SAID NOTHING.
"AND THEN HE WOULD GIVE EACH OF THEM A GIFT. AND AFTERWARD HE WOULD LEAVE THEIR LIVES ONCE MORE, THIS TIME FOR GOOD.
"IT WAS A FINE DREAM.

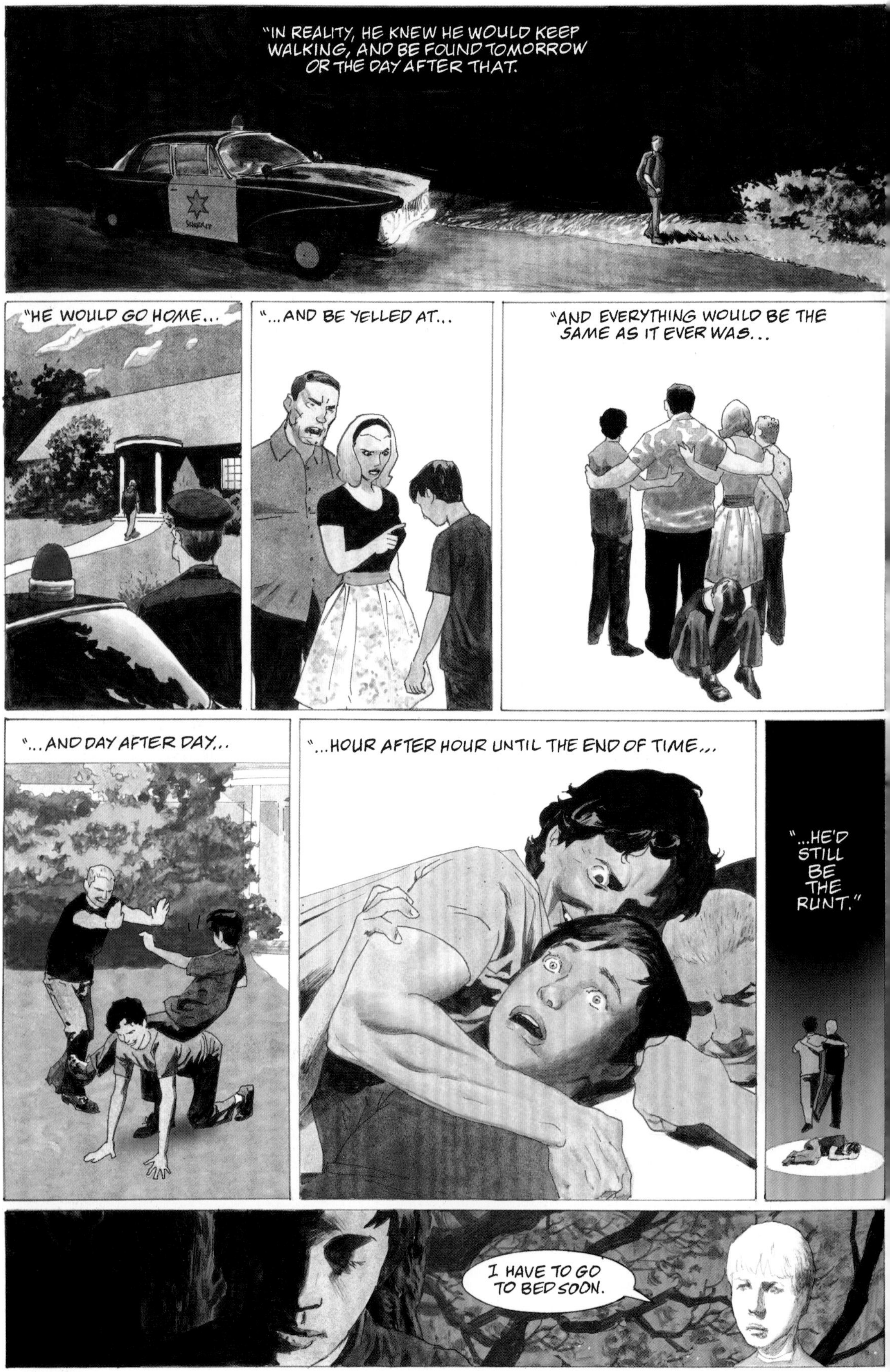
"IN REALITY, HE KNEW HE WOULD KEEP WALKING, AND BE FOUND TOMORROW OR THE DAY AFTER THAT.
"HE WOULD GO HOME...
"...AND BE YELLED AT...
"AND EVERYTHING WOULD BE THE SAME AS IT EVER WAS...
"...AND DAY AFTER DAY...
"...HOUR AFTER HOUR UNTIL THE END OF TIME...
"...HE'D STILL BE THE RUNT."
I HAVE TO GO TO BED SOON.

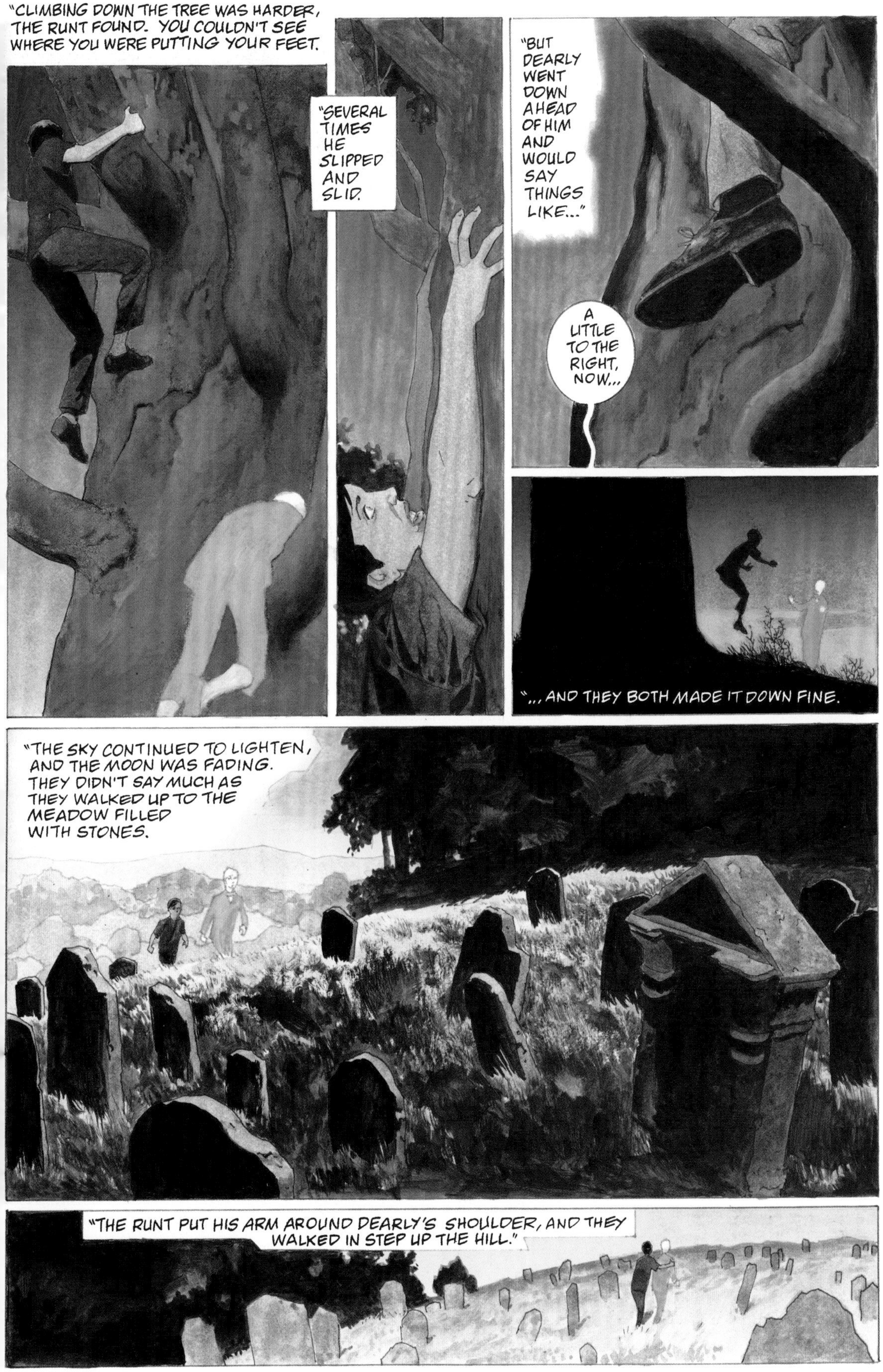
"CLIMBING DOWN THE TREE WAS HARDER, THE RUNT FOUND. YOU COULDN'T SEE WHERE YOU WERE PUTTING YOUR FEET.
"SEVERAL TIMES HE SLIPPED AND SLID.
"BUT DEARLY WENT DOWN AHEAD OF HIM AND WOULD SAY THINGS LIKE..."
A LITTLE TO THE RIGHT, NOW...
"...AND THEY BOTH MADE IT DOWN FINE.
"THE SKY CONTINUED TO LIGHTEN, AND THE MOON WAS FADING. THEY DIDN'T SAY MUCH AS THEY WALKED UP TO THE MEADOW FILLED WITH STONES.
"THE RUNT PUT HIS ARM AROUND DEARLY'S SHOULDER, AND THEY WALKED IN STEP UP THE HILL."

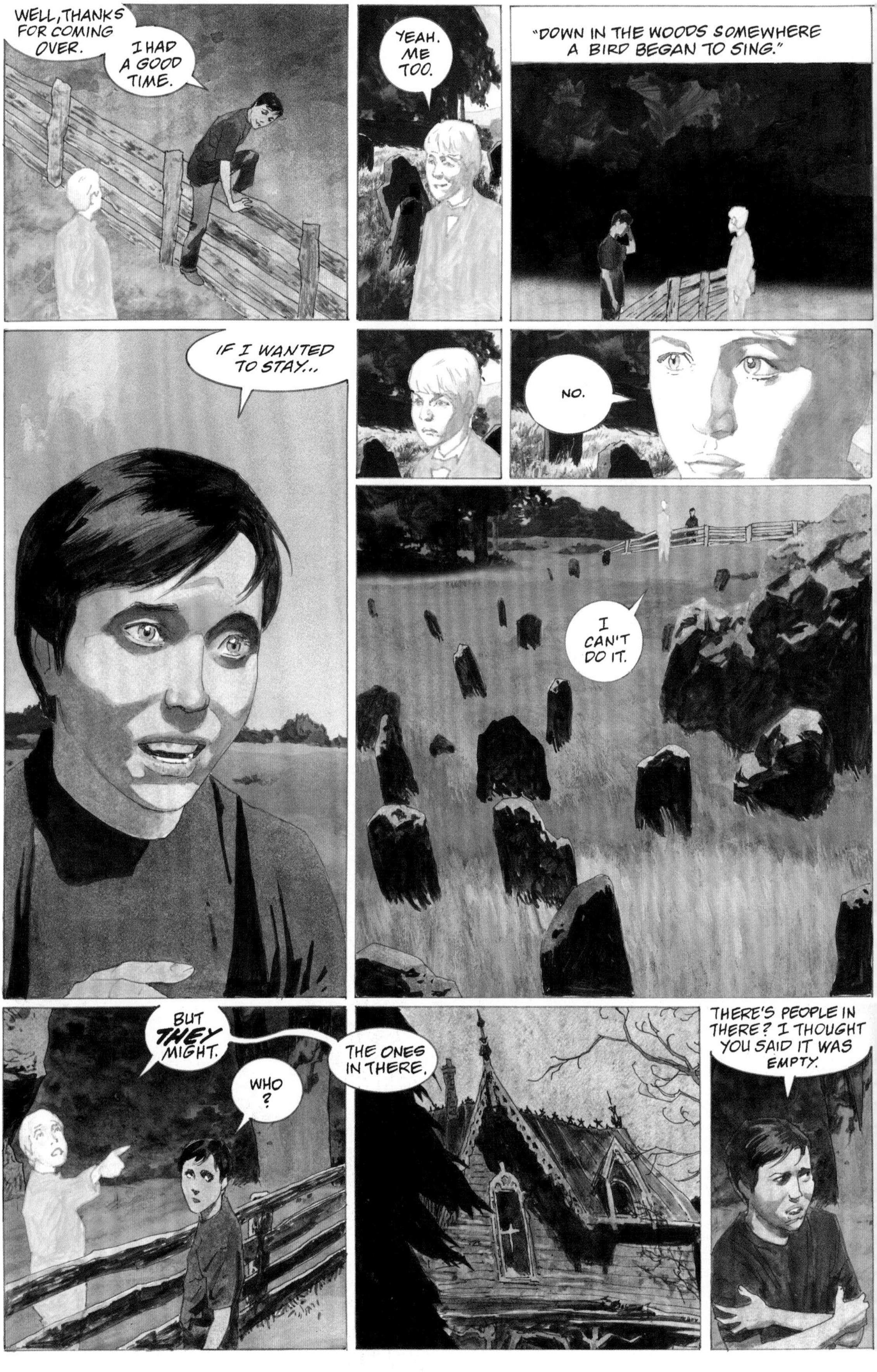
WELL, THANKS FOR COMING OVER.
I HAD A GOOD TIME.
YEAH. ME TOO.
"DOWN IN THE WOODS SOMEWHERE A BIRD BEGAN TO SING."
IF I WANTED TO STAY...
NO.
I CAN'T DO IT.
BUT THEY MIGHT.
WHO?
THE ONES IN THERE.
THERE'S PEOPLE IN THERE? I THOUGHT YOU SAID IT WAS EMPTY.

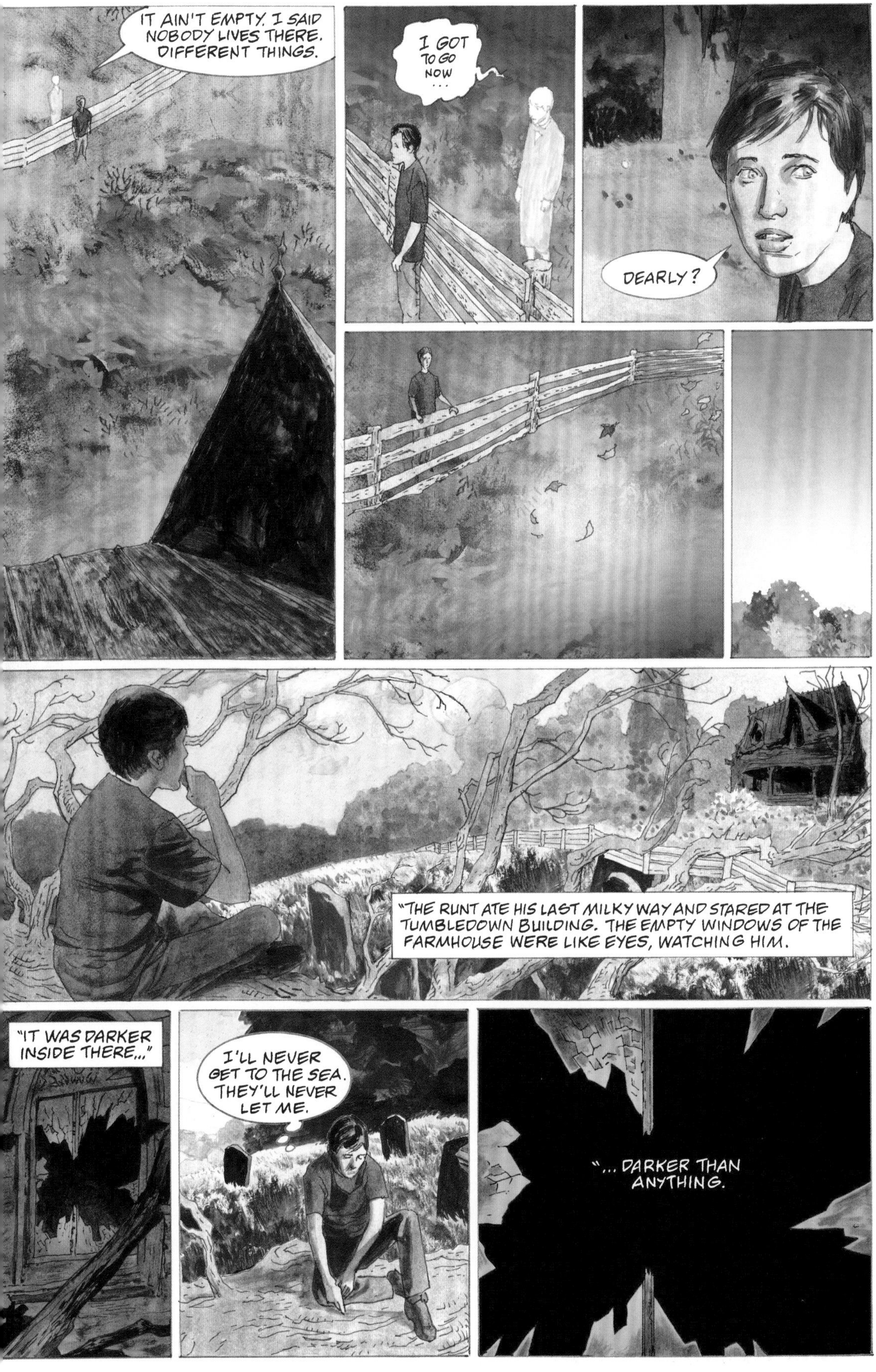
IT AIN'T EMPTY. I SAID NOBODY LIVES THERE. DIFFERENT THINGS.
I GOT TO GO NOW . . .
DEARLY?
"THE RUNT ATE HIS LAST MILKY WAY AND STARED AT THE TUMBLEDOWN BUILDING. THE EMPTY WINDOWS OF THE FARMHOUSE WERE LIKE EYES, WATCHING HIM.
"IT WAS DARKER INSIDE THERE..."
I'LL NEVER GET TO THE SEA. THEY'LL NEVER LET ME.
"... DARKER THAN ANYTHING.

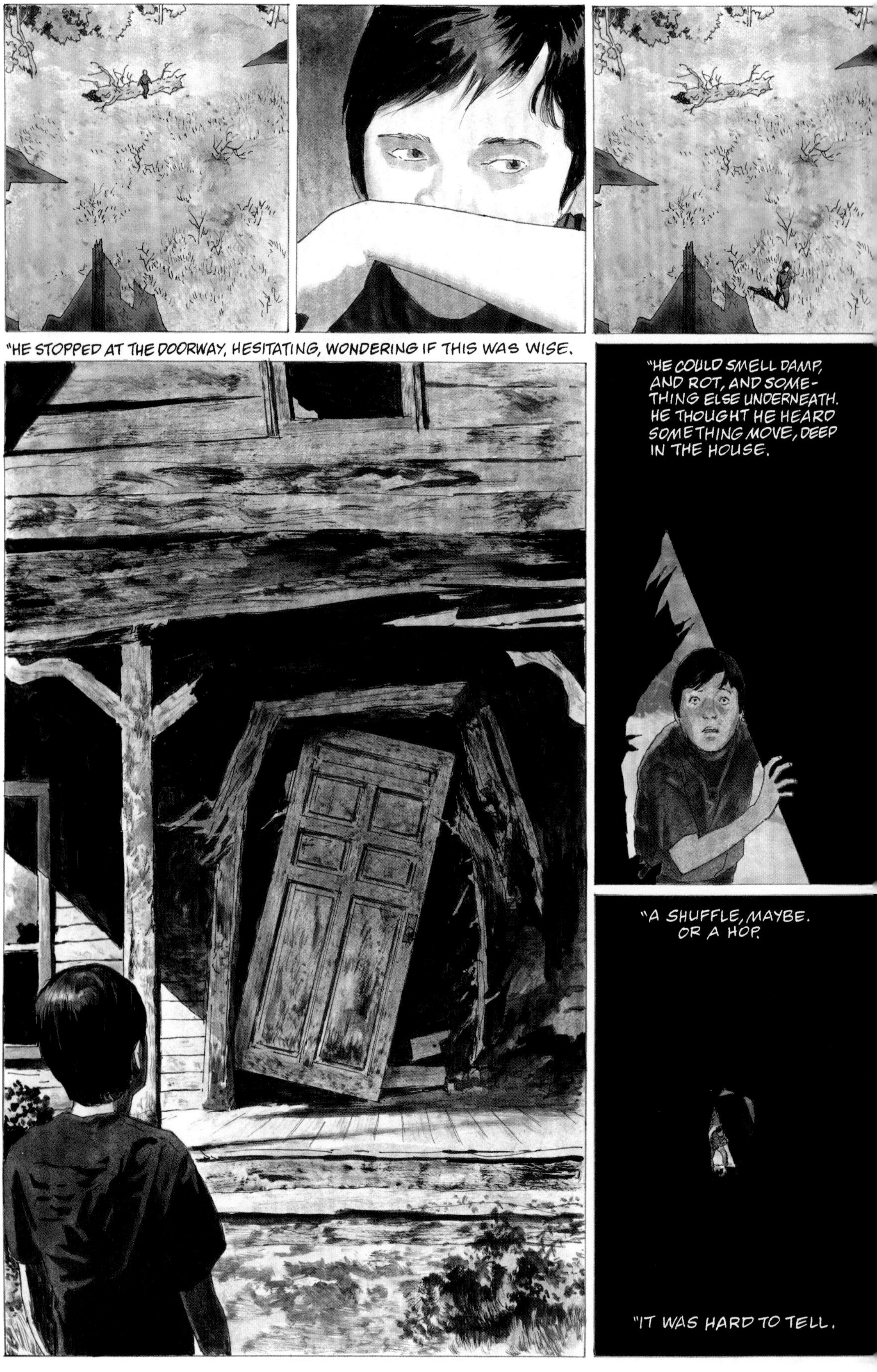
"HE STOPPED AT THE DOORWAY, HESITATING, WONDERING IF THIS WAS WISE.
"HE COULD SMELL DAMP, AND ROT, AND SOMETHING ELSE UNDERNEATH. HE THOUGHT HE HEARD SOMETHING MOVE, DEEP IN THE HOUSE.
"A SHUFFLE, MAYBE. OR A HOP.
"IT WAS HARD TO TELL.

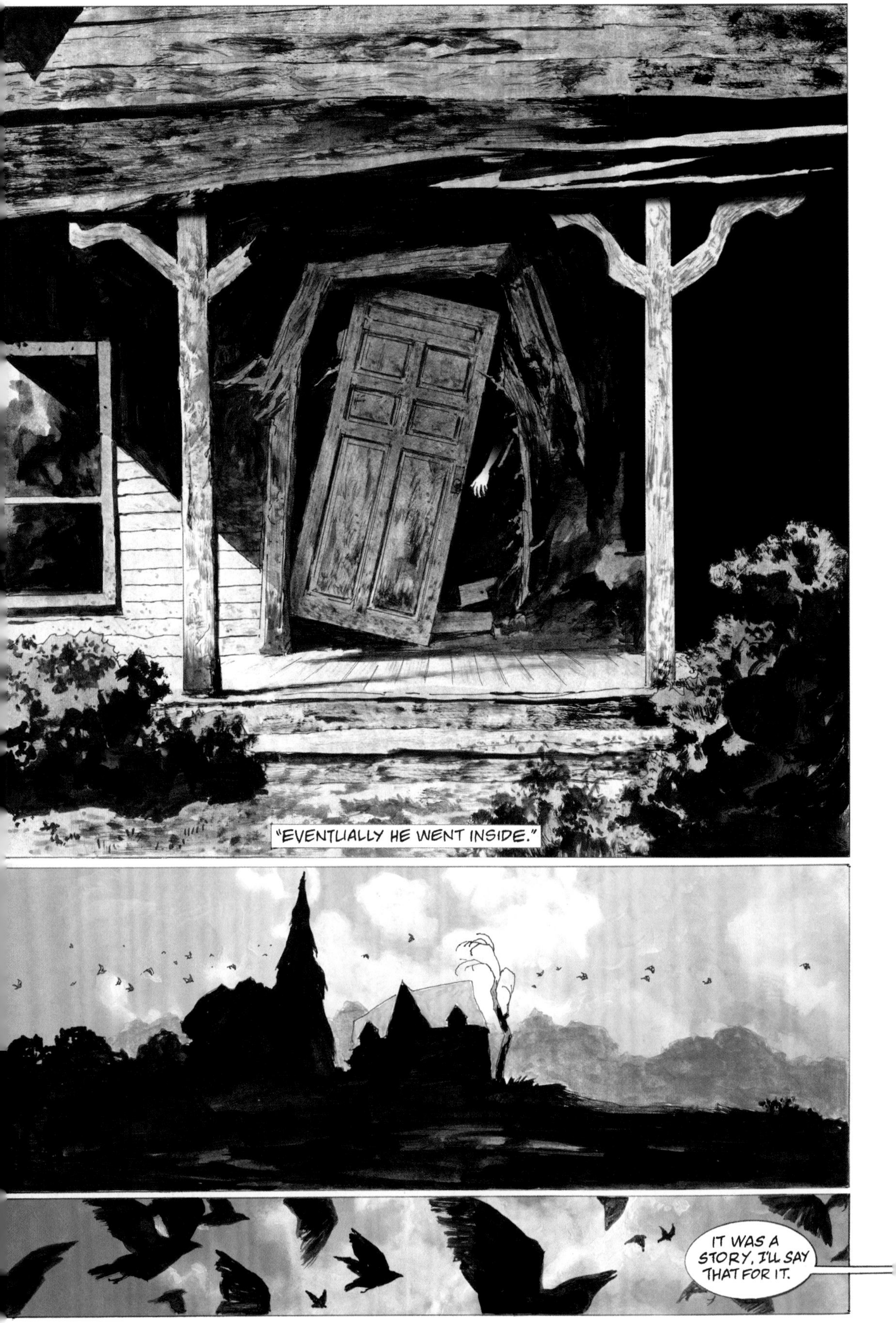
"EVENTUALLY HE WENT INSIDE."
IT WAS A STORY, I'LL SAY THAT FOR IT.

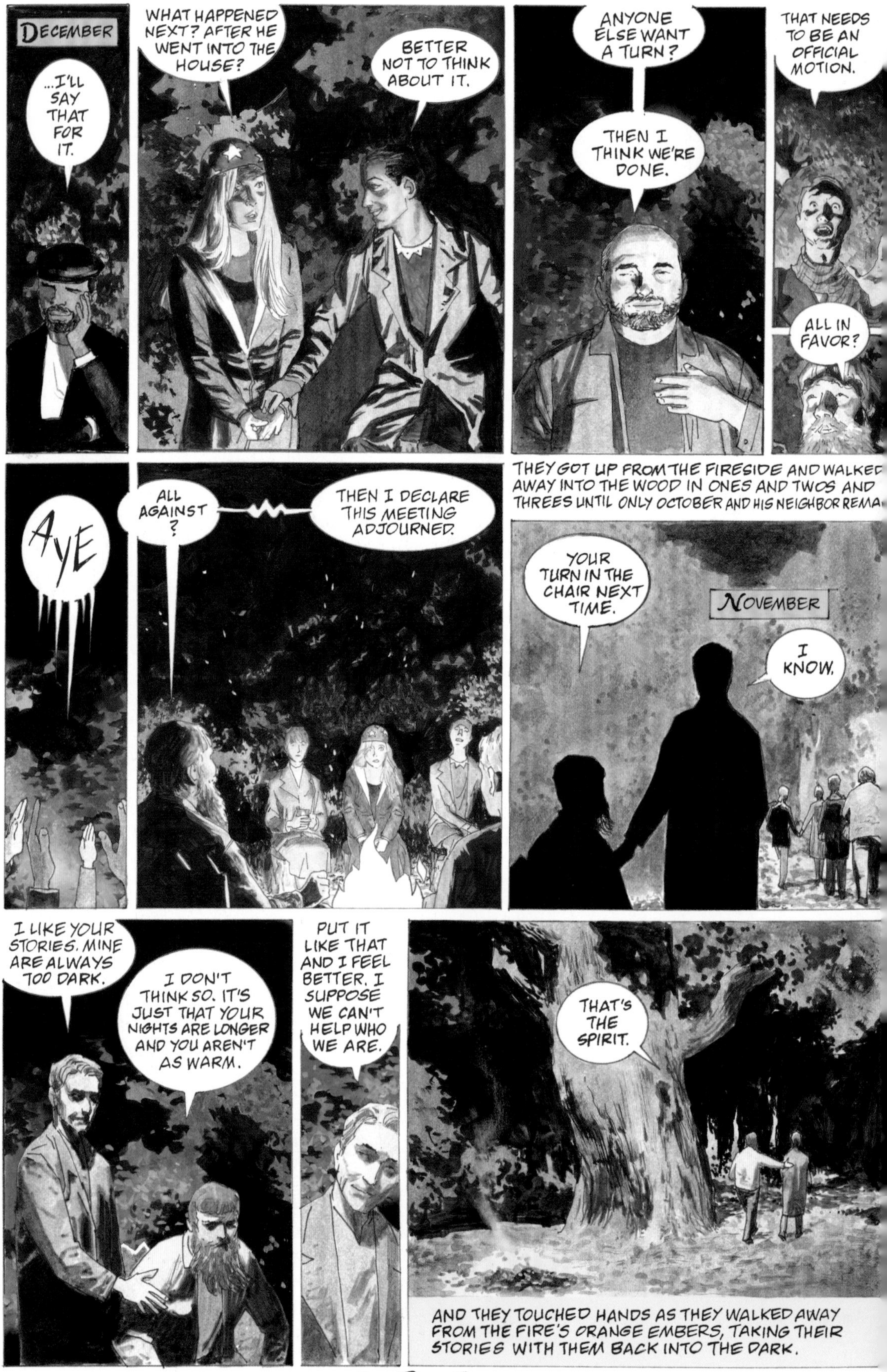
DECEMBER
...I'LL SAY THAT FOR IT.
WHAT HAPPENED NEXT? AFTER HE WENT INTO THE HOUSE?
BETTER NOT TO THINK ABOUT IT.
ANYONE ELSE WANT A TURN?
THEN I THINK WE'RE DONE.
THAT NEEDS TO BE AN OFFICIAL MOTION.
ALL IN FAVOR?
AYE
ALL AGAINST?
THEN I DECLARE THIS MEETING ADJOURNED.
THEY GOT UP FROM THE FIRESIDE AND WALKED AWAY INTO THE WOOD IN ONES AND TWOS AND THREES UNTIL ONLY OCTOBER AND HIS NEIGHBOR REMA
YOUR TURN IN THE CHAIR NEXT TIME.
NOVEMBER
I KNOW.
I LIKE YOUR STORIES. MINE ARE ALWAYS TOO DARK.
I DON'T THINK SO. IT'S JUST THAT YOUR NIGHTS ARE LONGER AND YOU AREN'T AS WARM.
PUT IT LIKE THAT AND I FEEL BETTER. I SUPPOSE WE CAN'T HELP WHO WE ARE.
THAT'S THE SPIRIT.
AND THEY TOUCHED HANDS AS THEY WALKED AWAY FROM THE FIRE'S ORANGE EMBERS, TAKING THEIR STORIES WITH THEM BACK INTO THE DARK.

FOR RAY BRADBURY

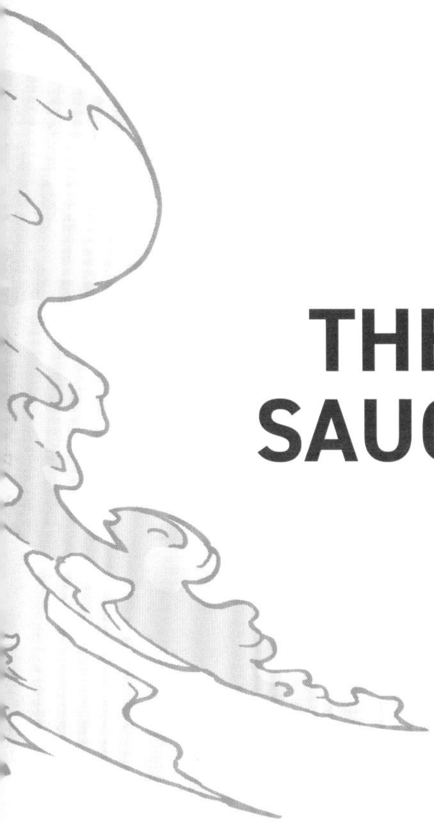

THE DAY THE SAUCERS CAME

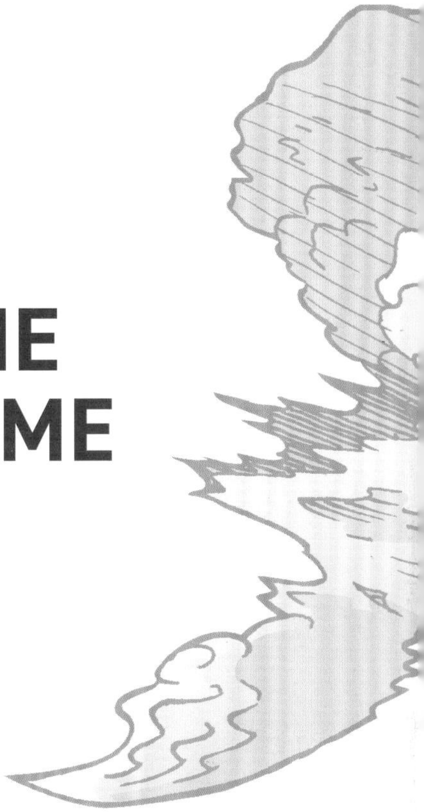

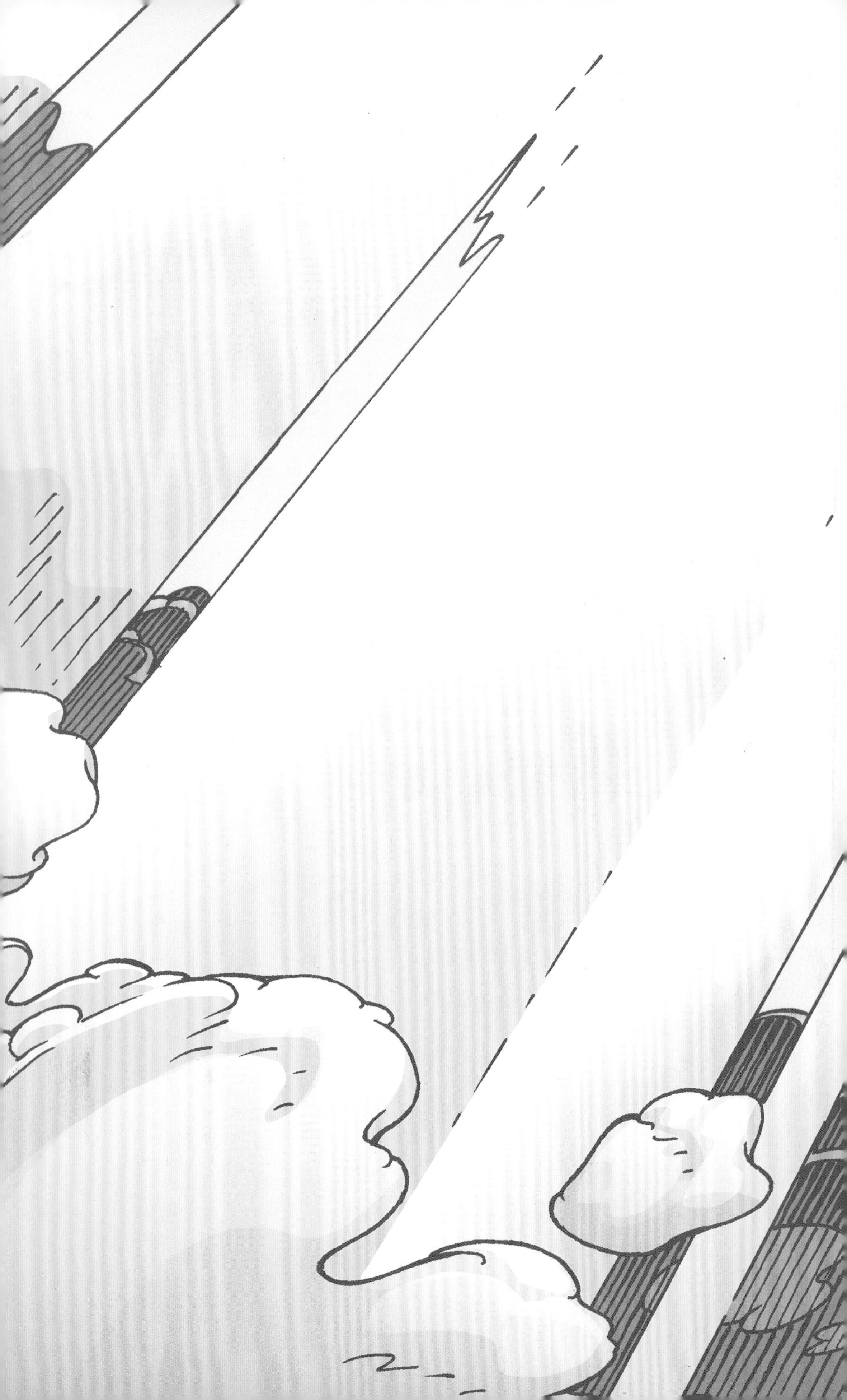

THE DAY THE SAUCERS CAME

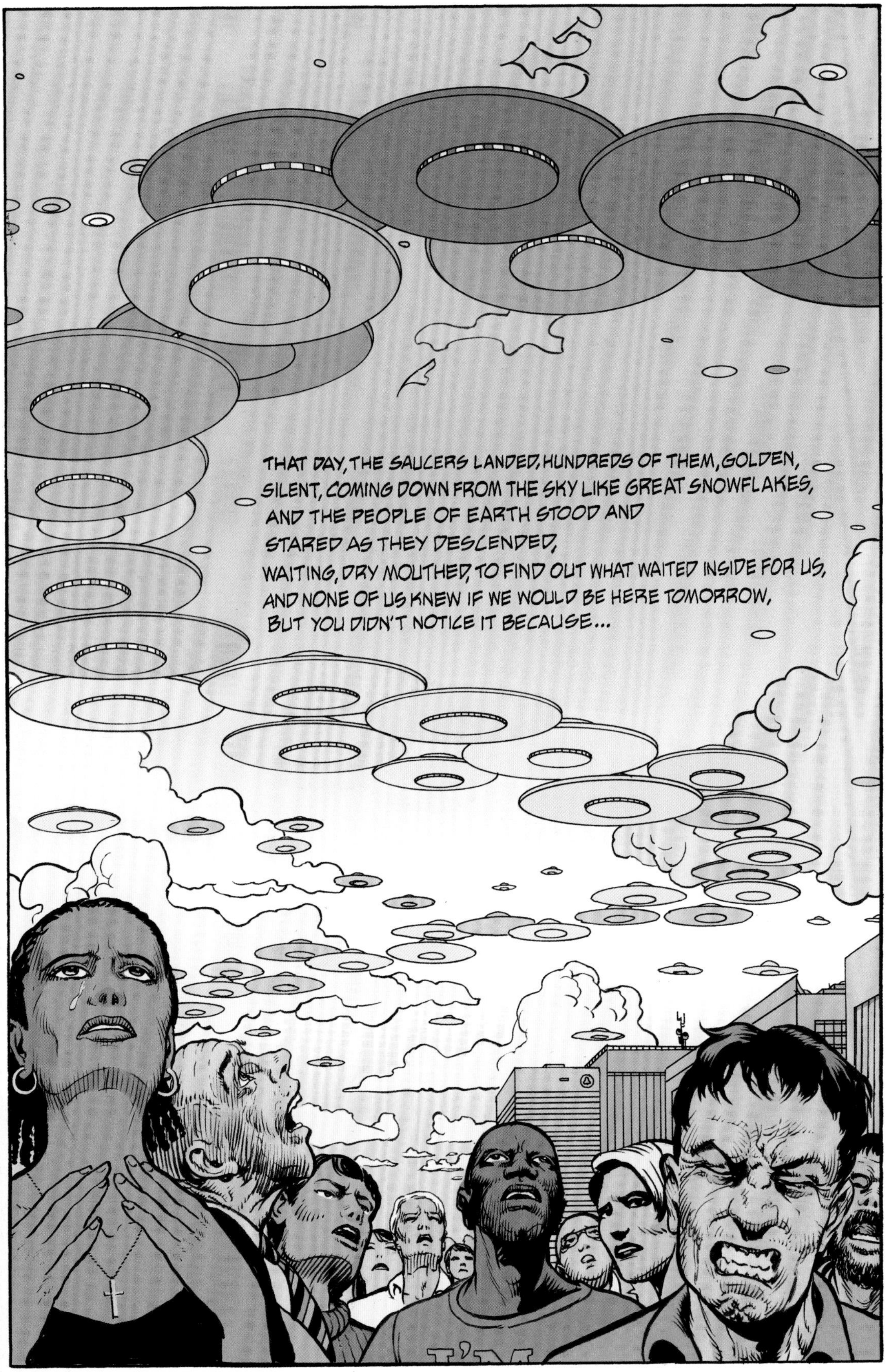
THAT DAY, THE SAUCERS LANDED. HUNDREDS OF THEM, GOLDEN, SILENT, COMING DOWN FROM THE SKY LIKE GREAT SNOWFLAKES, AND THE PEOPLE OF EARTH STOOD AND STARED AS THEY DESCENDED, WAITING, DRY MOUTHED, TO FIND OUT WHAT WAITED INSIDE FOR US, AND NONE OF US KNEW IF WE WOULD BE HERE TOMORROW, BUT YOU DIDN'T NOTICE IT BECAUSE...

Story by **Neil Gaiman** Art by **Paul Chadwick** Lettering by **Gaspar Saladino**

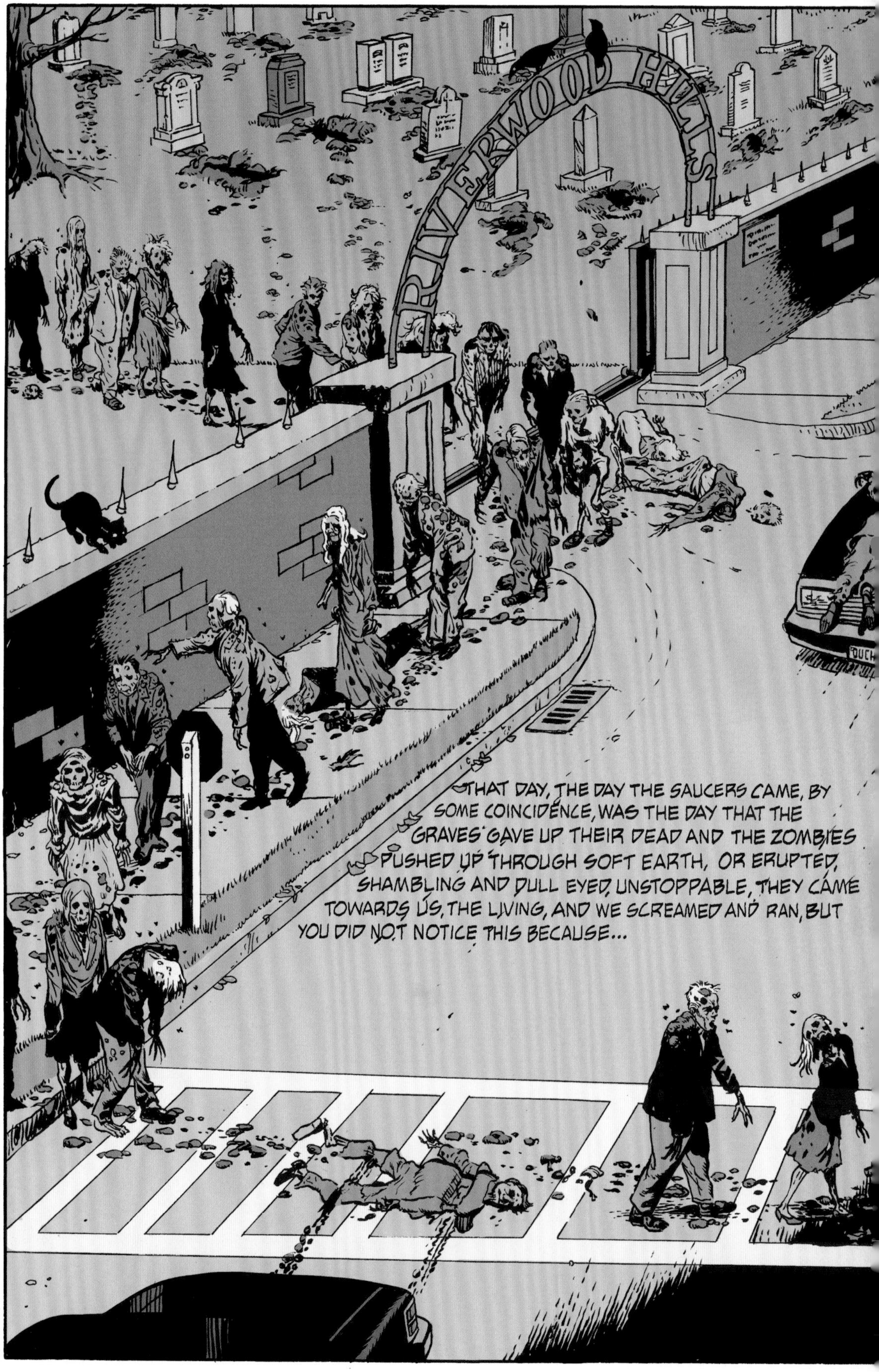
RIVERWOOD HILLS
THAT DAY, THE DAY THE SAUCERS CAME, BY SOME COINCIDENCE, WAS THE DAY THAT THE GRAVES GAVE UP THEIR DEAD AND THE ZOMBIES PUSHED UP THROUGH SOFT EARTH, OR ERUPTED, SHAMBLING AND DULL EYED, UNSTOPPABLE, THEY CAME TOWARDS US, THE LIVING, AND WE SCREAMED AND RAN, BUT YOU DID NOT NOTICE THIS BECAUSE...

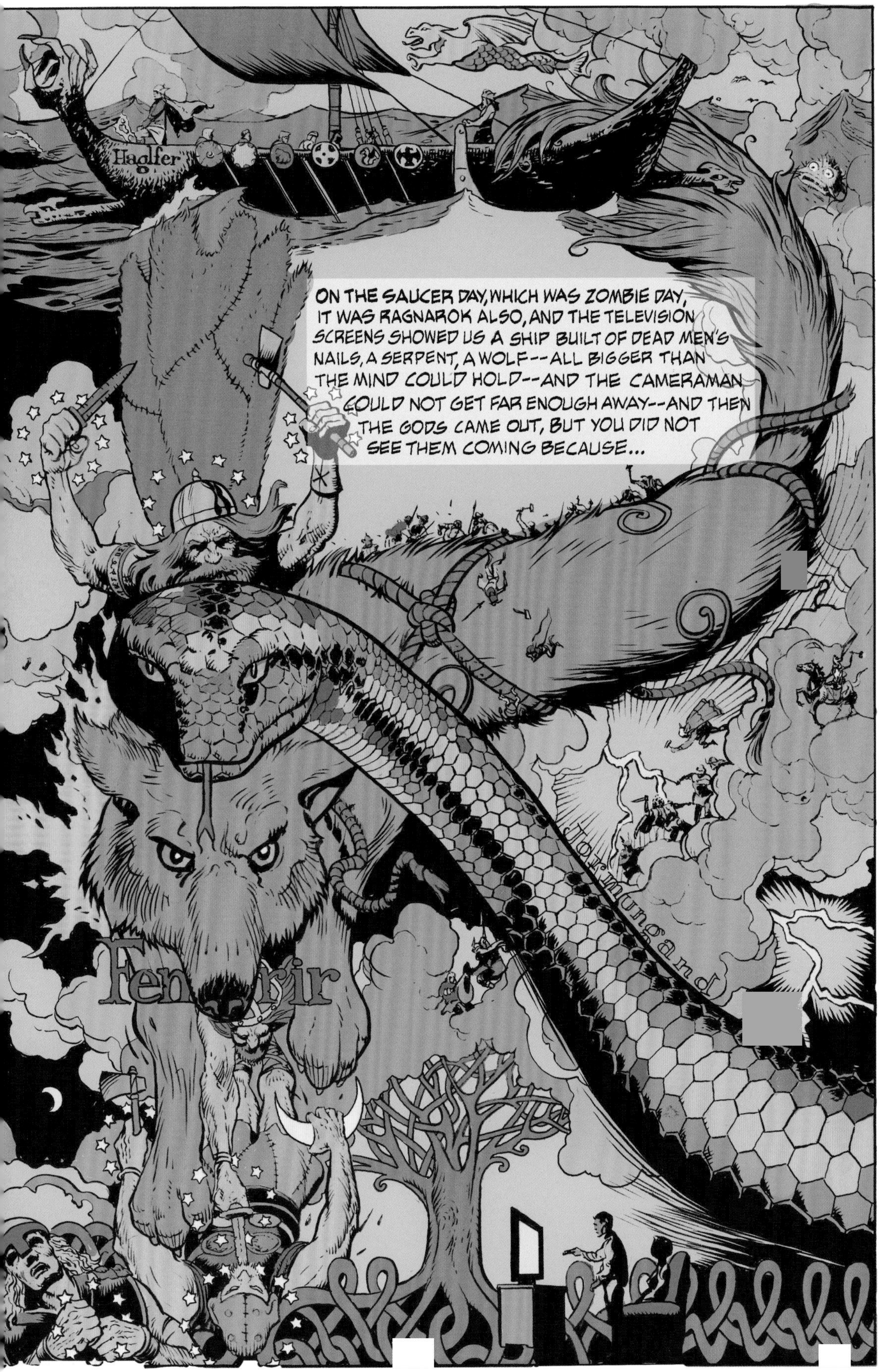
Haglfer
ON THE SAUCER DAY, WHICH WAS ZOMBIE DAY, IT WAS RAGNAROK ALSO, AND THE TELEVISION SCREENS SHOWED US A SHIP BUILT OF DEAD MEN'S NAILS, A SERPENT, A WOLF--ALL BIGGER THAN THE MIND COULD HOLD--AND THE CAMERAMAN COULD NOT GET FAR ENOUGH AWAY--AND THEN THE GODS CAME OUT, BUT YOU DID NOT SEE THEM COMING BECAUSE...
Jormungand
Fenrir

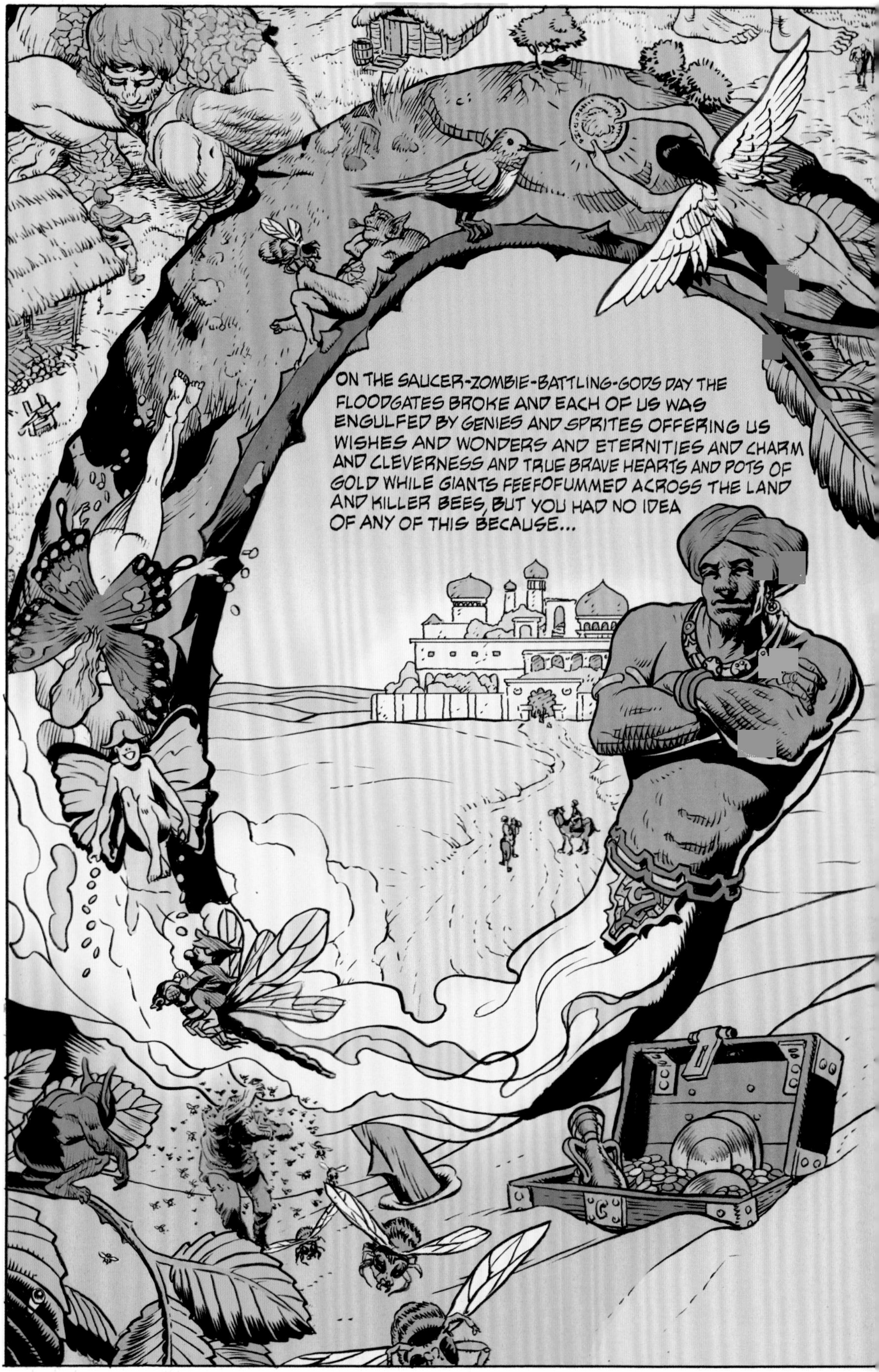
ON THE SAUCER-ZOMBIE-BATTLING-GODS DAY THE FLOODGATES BROKE AND EACH OF US WAS ENGULFED BY GENIES AND SPRITES OFFERING US WISHES AND WONDERS AND ETERNITIES AND CHARM AND CLEVERNESS AND TRUE BRAVE HEARTS AND POTS OF GOLD WHILE GIANTS FEEFOFUMMED ACROSS THE LAND AND KILLER BEES, BUT YOU HAD NO IDEA OF ANY OF THIS BECAUSE...

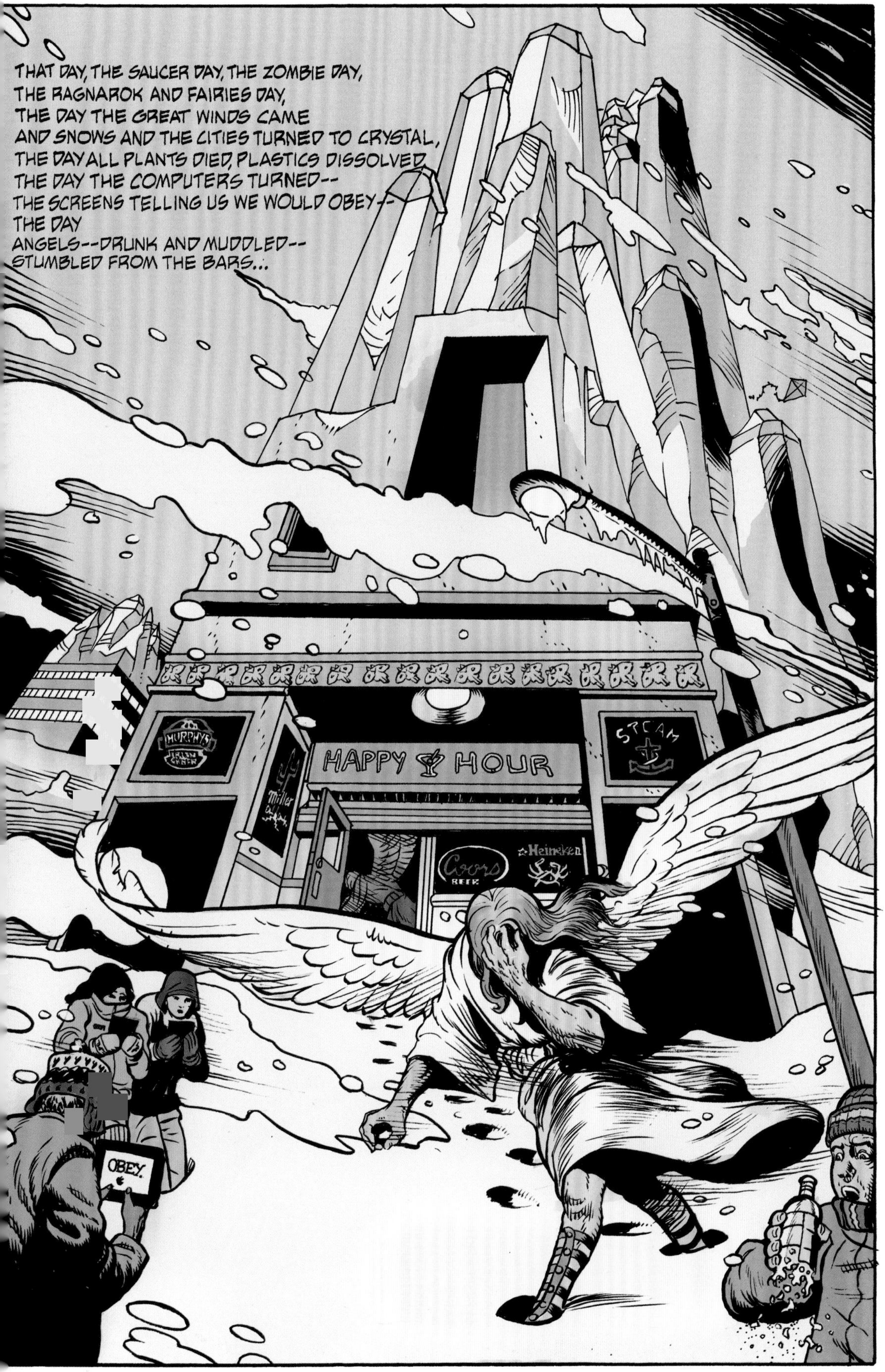
THAT DAY, THE SAUCER DAY, THE ZOMBIE DAY,
THE RAGNAROK AND FAIRIES DAY,
THE DAY THE GREAT WINDS CAME
AND SNOWS AND THE CITIES TURNED TO CRYSTAL,
THE DAY ALL PLANTS DIED, PLASTICS DISSOLVED,
THE DAY THE COMPUTERS TURNED--
THE SCREENS TELLING US WE WOULD OBEY--
THE DAY
ANGELS--DRUNK AND MUDDLED--
STUMBLED FROM THE BARS...
MURPHY'S
HAPPY HOUR
STEAM
Miller
Coors BEER
Heineken
OBEY.

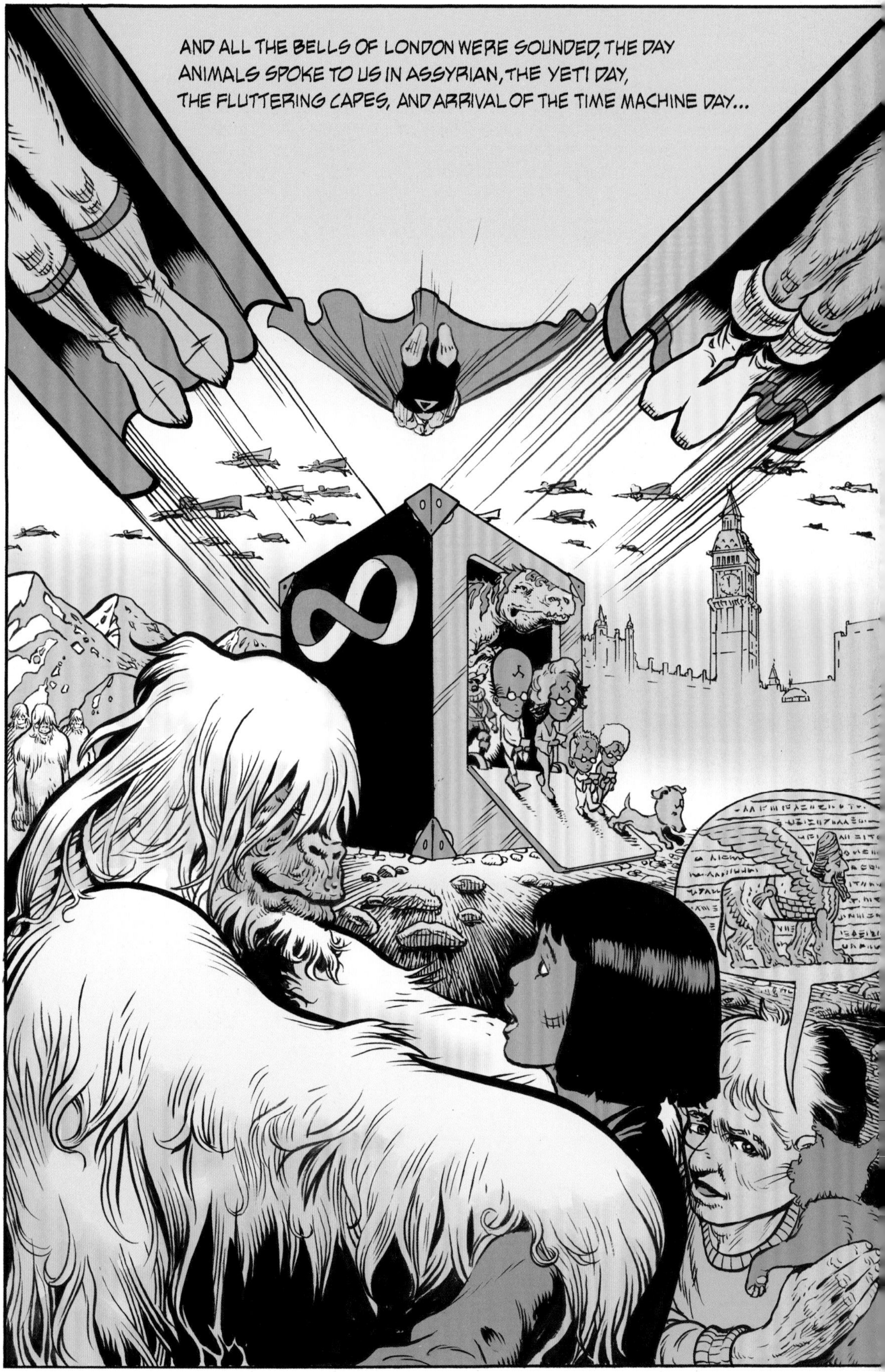
AND ALL THE BELLS OF LONDON WERE SOUNDED, THE DAY
ANIMALS SPOKE TO US IN ASSYRIAN, THE YETI DAY,
THE FLUTTERING CAPES, AND ARRIVAL OF THE TIME MACHINE DAY...

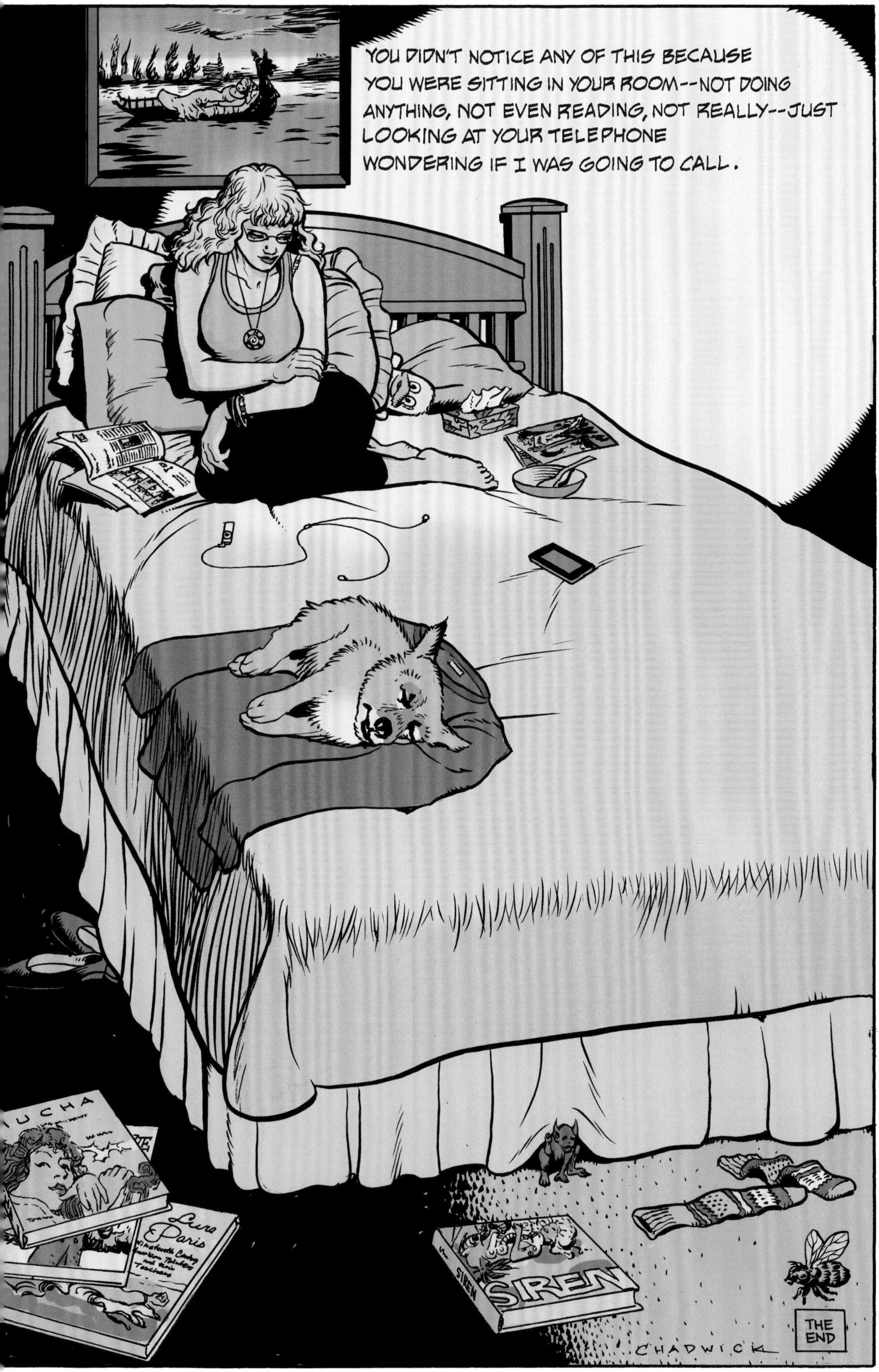
YOU DIDN'T NOTICE ANY OF THIS BECAUSE YOU WERE SITTING IN YOUR ROOM--NOT DOING ANYTHING, NOT EVEN READING, NOT REALLY--JUST LOOKING AT YOUR TELEPHONE WONDERING IF I WAS GOING TO CALL.
SIREN
CHADWICK
THE END

MORE TITLES FROM

THE
NEIL GAIMAN
LIBRARY

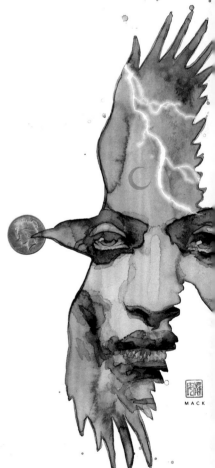

THE FACTS IN THE CASE OF THE DEPARTURE OF MISS FINCH
2nd Edition
Neil Gaiman and Michael Zulli
$13.99 | 978-1-61655-949-6

NEIL GAIMAN'S HOW TO TALK TO GIRLS AT PARTIES
Neil Gaiman, Fábio Moon, and Gabriel Bá
$17.99 | ISBN 978-1-61655-955-7

NEIL GAIMAN'S TROLL BRIDGE
Neil Gaiman and Colleen Doran
$14.99 | ISBN 978-1-50670-008-3

FORBIDDEN BRIDES OF THE FACELESS SLAVES IN THE SECRET HOUSE OF THE NIGHT OF DREAD DESIRE
Neil Gaiman and Shane Oakley
$17.99 | ISBN 978-1-50670-140-0

CREATURES OF THE NIGHT
2nd Edition
Neil Gaiman and Michael Zulli
$12.99 | ISBN 978-1-50670-025-0

SIGNAL TO NOISE
Neil Gaiman and Dave McKean
$24.99 | ISBN 978-1-59307-752-5

HARLEQUIN VALENTINE
2nd Edition
Neil Gaiman and John Bolton
$12.99 | ISBN 978-1-50670-087-8

AMERICAN GODS: SHADOWS
Neil Gaiman, P. Craig Russell, Scott Hampton, and others
$29.99 | ISBN 978-1-50670-386-2

NEIL GAIMAN'S A STUDY IN EMERALD
Neil Gaiman and Rafael Albuquerque
$17.99 | ISBN 978-1-50670-393-0

THE PROBLEM OF SUSAN AND OTHER STORIES
Neil Gaiman, P. Craig Russell, Paul Chadwick, and others
$17.99 | ISBN 978-1-50670-511-8

MACK

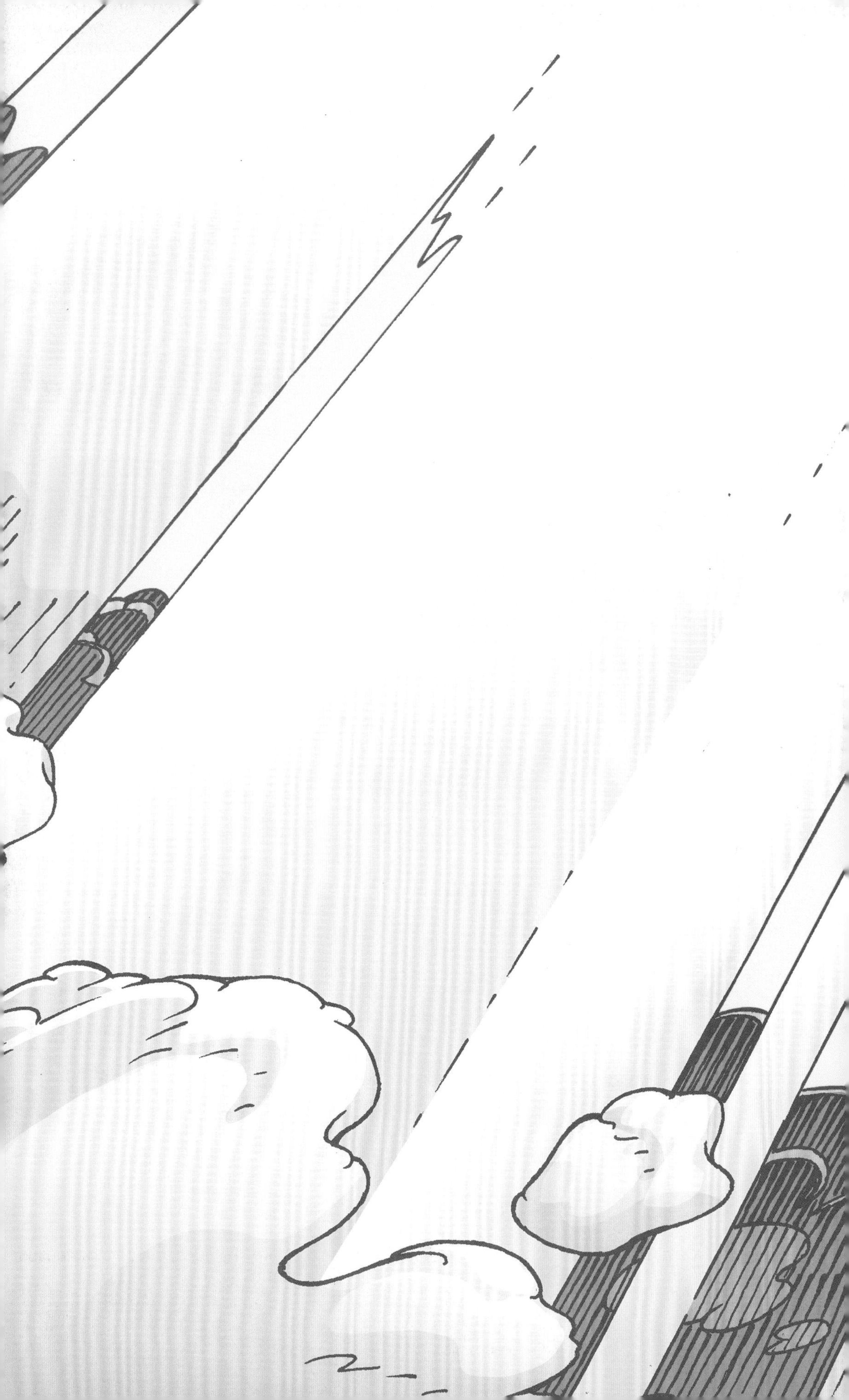

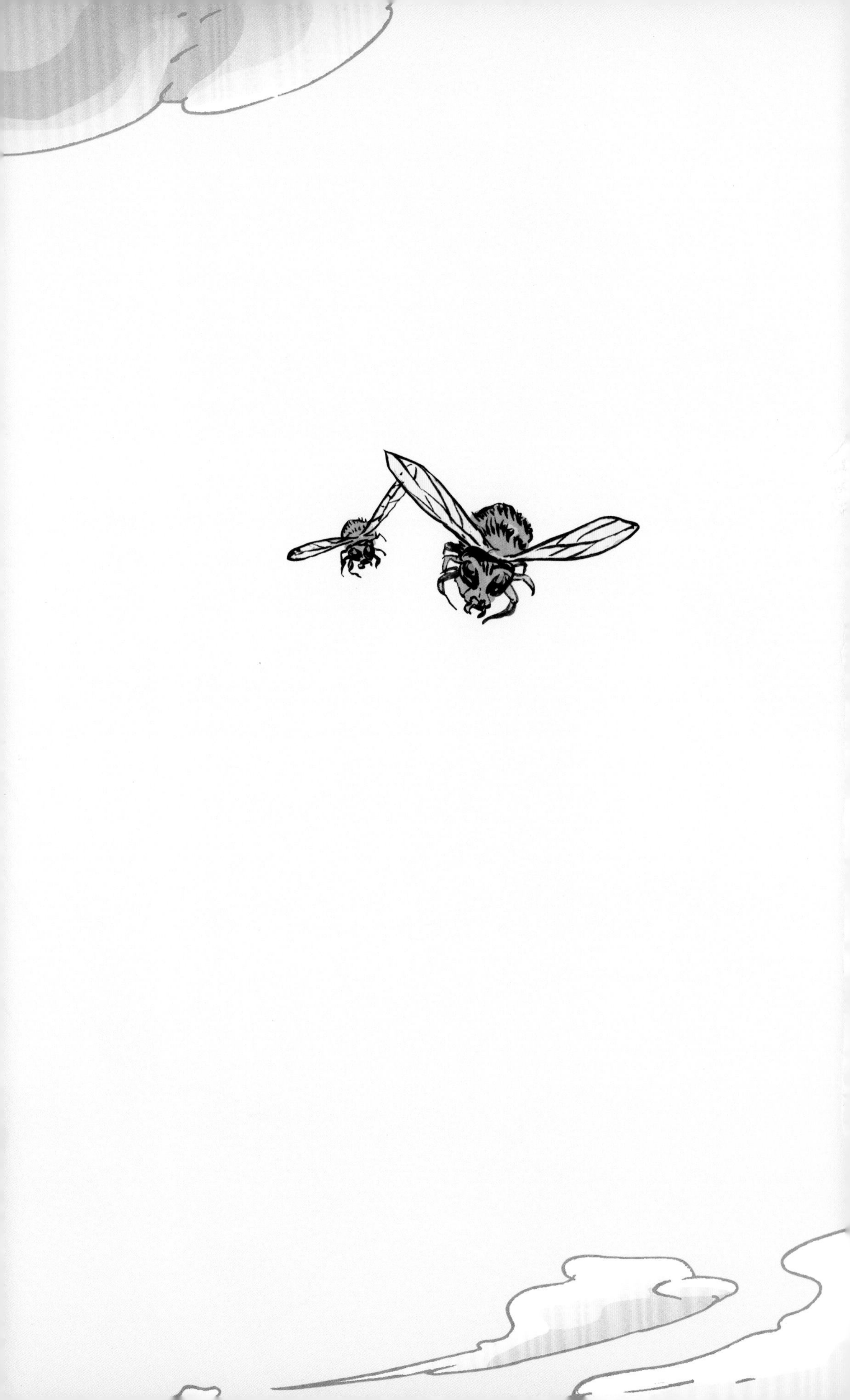

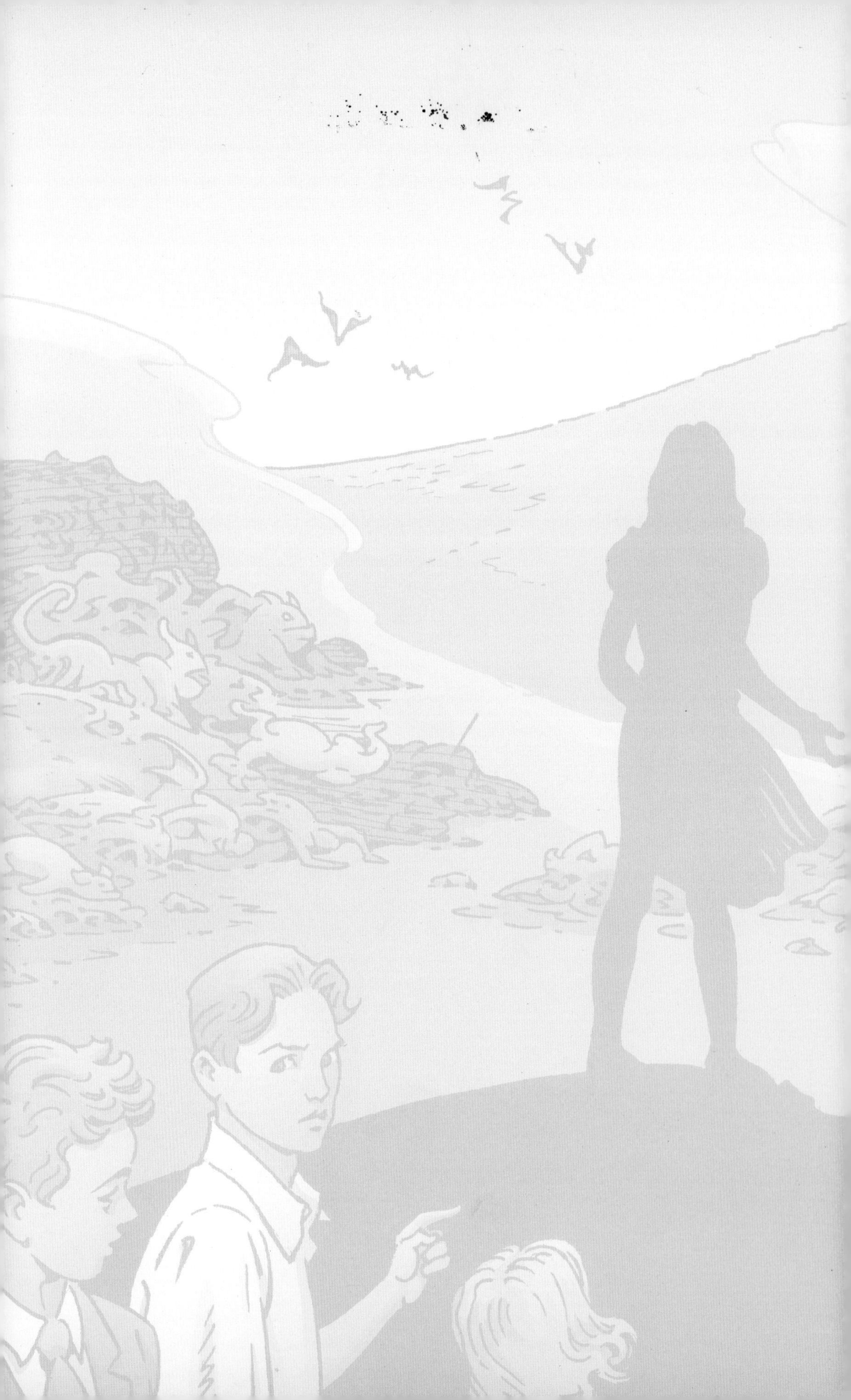